DESTINATION MARKETING INSIGHTS

DESTINATION MARKETING INSIGHTS

HOW TO BOOST PERFORMANCE, INCREASE CUSTOMERS, AND MAXIMIZE MARKET SHARE

Marshall E. Murdaugh

"Marshall Murdaugh is the dean of destination marketing."
–John Boatright, Chairman Emeritus,
Association of Travel Marketing Executives

MILL CITY PRESS, MINNEAPOLIS

Mill City Press, Inc.
212 3rd Avenue North, Suite 290
Minneapolis, MN 55401
612.455.2294
www.millcitypublishing.com

Copies of *Destination Marketing Insights* may be ordered at
www.MMTourismMarketing.com or www.Amazon.com.

Special thanks to Wil Brewer, president of Performance-Solutions-Group, Inc., for his input on "How to Hire, Fire, and Manage."

Editorial support provided by Editorial Inspirations, www.editorialinspirations.com.

Marshall Murdaugh can be reached at mmurdaughmktg@aol.com or at www.MMTourismMarketing.com.

ISBN-13: 978-1-938223-38-9
LCCN: 2012939150

Book Design by Mary Nelson

Printed in the United States of America

DEDICATION

To my mother, Dorothy "Dot" Murdaugh, who taught me how to live with gusto, a strong work ethic, an inquisitive nature, and an abundance of optimism.

To my sons, Marshall and Reese, who've made me consistently proud.

Special thanks to those who helped hone my ideas, perceptions, and skills through the sharing of their own special expertise, dreams, and successes: Uncle Reese Fogarty, many of my DMO leadership (Donald Trump, George Steinbrenner, Percy Sutton, Jeff Sanford, Harry Miller, Dick Ashman, Brad Smith, Marvin Sutherland, Charles "Chris" A. Christopherson, Fred W. Walker, and Jack C. Smith), Cynthia Ham, John Tigrett, David Porter, Dr. Douglas Frechtling, Dr. Suzanne Cook, John Boatright, Doug Talley, Pamela Fiori, Wes Westley, Ed Beck, Ben Pope, Anne Daly Heller, George Woltz, Dave Martin, Bob Peattie, John Goodwin, Leah Woolford, Donovan Shia, Bob Whitley, Maggie Megee, Dan Bartges, and many others.

CONTENTS

FOREWORD

By Kevin Kane, Chairman, Destination Marketing Association International (fiscal year 2011–12), and President & CEO, Memphis Convention and Visitors Bureau

I first met and got to know Marshall Murdaugh in my hometown of Memphis when I was a senior executive with the Holiday Corporation and he was continuing a storied career as one of the industry's most successful destination marketing organization CEOs—first as Virginia's state tourism commissioner, then as president of the Memphis and New York City Convention and Visitor Bureaus and the Atlantic City Convention and Visitors Authority.

Because Marshall's core expertise was destination marketing, he quickly became a popular, sought-after consultant to many domestic and international destinations for strategic planning and performance enhancement. And he was, therefore, Destination Marketing Association International's easy choice for producing the marketing section in our ground-breaking industry textbook, *Fundamentals of Destination Management and Marketing.*

After college and prior to entering the tourism industry, Marshall had some diverse and interesting experiences. He was a member of the production team for Virginia's first public television station and later sports, weather, and weekend news anchor for Virginia's CBS television affiliate, before being selected as public affairs officer for local county government. Next, he was tapped as public relations manager for *Fortune* 500's Reynolds Metals Company where he worked as the public relations manager for product development and market research, as well as on America's first Earth Day and the Canadian–American Circuit's Team McLaren Formula 1 racing program—all exciting stuff.

Finally, at age thirty, Marshall became the youngest state tourism director in the country when he landed the pivotal job as Virginia's Tourism Commissioner that would later define him for so many. "The agency was in the initial phase of developing the new 'Virginia Is for Lovers' theme," Marshall explained, "and I found myself in the right place at the right time—an accidental occurrence that's happened quite often throughout my career." Well, perhaps. But it was then that Marshall took that advertising theme line and created the wildly successful, lovers integrated marketing campaign that won national industry recognition and the top award from the Travel Industry Association of America.

The rest is history. Today, we are all the beneficiaries of Marshall's significant expertise in the field of destination marketing, grounded in thirty-five years of marketing development for more than eighty of the industry's most successful destination programs.

I've discovered in Marshall a good friend, generous with sharing his knowledge and insights. When I stepped into the role of chief executive at the Memphis CVB, I found Marshall's imprint throughout our promotional activities and strategies. His previous campaign for our city had become local legend. He gave me great advice in my own quest to launch a new brand and create a strong economic engine from Memphis's many diverse amenities and hospitality services. Today, Marshall's marketing expertise still serves my local industry as well as the international tourism community that is Destination Marketing Association International.

He has titled this book *Destination Marketing Insights*—an apt description, I believe, from such a truly insightful marketing strategist. I know you'll enjoy and profit from it—and from Marshall as well.

INTRODUCTION

Insight (in-sahyt) – noun
1. An instance of apprehending the true nature of a thing, especially through intuitive understanding
2. Penetrating mental vision or discernment; the faculty of seeing into inner character or underlying truth
3. In psychology:
a. understanding of relationships that sheds light on or helps solve a problem
b. understanding of the motivational forces behind one's actions, thoughts, or behavior; self-knowledge

The American Marketing Association defines marketing as "the activity, set of institutions and processes for creating, communicating, delivering and exchanging offerings that have value for customers, clients, partners and society at large." For our purposes, marketing can be succinctly described as "the process of determining customer needs and then filling them."

Although tourism marketing is grounded in the foundation of consumer behavior and the research that defines it, it is insight—particularly through intuitive understandings—that plays such an important role in applying research findings and determining pragmatic directions, creative applications, and business practices that can deliver optimal destination marketing opportunities. Thus, the insights that I've gained from a lifetime of experiences in successful destination marketing, as well as management, are what this book is all about.

Just a few of the highlights you're about to read include the following:

- convention sales case histories that can boost annual business by at least 25 percent a year
- new funding plans that have increased CVB marketing budgets by up to 300 percent
- review and analysis of the emerging new leisure trend known as experiential travel—which more than four of ten travelers are now participating in—and how destinations can best apply it for motivating even more visitors
- Internet methodologies that reliably produce more than a 40-to-1 return-on-investment for destinations in new visitors and economic impact.

Today, most readers of this book have long recognized what millions of other people around the world are beginning to acknowledge: the once-thought invisible business of tourism has become one the world's largest industries, fueling the economies of local, state, regional, and national governments in all but some third-world countries. And even there, it provides the brightest hope for economic growth, opportunity, and stability.

Here in the United States, domestic and international visitor spending is an estimated $759 billion annually, employing 7.4 million industry people with a payroll exceeding $188 billion. But tourism clearly isn't like spontaneous combustion. It doesn't just happen. It has to be marketed, nurtured, and protected.

Guiding the growth of this industry are thousands of destination marketing organizations (or DMOs, known as tourism offices, convention and visitor bureaus, and similar descriptions). Yet they all share the same mission on behalf of their communities of business and government constituents: to market to travelers the benefits of visiting these areas, be they cities, counties, regional programs, states, or countries—and as a result, the production of substantial economic and social returns for the welfare of their constituent communities.

This book is not only for those destination marketing professionals who seek to produce greater shares of customer attention and business, but also for those with the vast and diverse hospitality business interests who, as stakeholders, wish to play a more effective role in these destination marketing tourism efforts.

They include, but certainly aren't limited to,

- the accommodations industry
- transportation and travel
- travel agents and tour companies
- restaurants
- retail trade
- events and attractions
- the cultural, heritage, and sports communities
- meeting and convention planners and other executives
- governments, which receive the substantial benefits of this burgeoning and sometimes misunderstood industry, including new and sustained jobs and the myriad of taxes generated from visitor spending.

Finally, for the academic community, this book seeks to provide the marketing power to know how to put strategic and tactical best practices to work that can achieve the highest performance success for tourism programs everywhere. Also included are key case studies and their significant results.

I'm really excited to finally bring this book to fruition. I hope you enjoy it, are challenged by the industry, and stay around to play a role in its continued evolution that means so much to so many.

Marshall Murdaugh

CHAPTER 1
Marketing

"The secret of success is to know something nobody else knows."
–Aristotle Onassis

Your Strategic Priority:
The DMO Mission, Value, and Vision

"Vision without action is a daydream. Action without vision is a night-mare," so states an old Japanese proverb. The initial strategic planning requirement for DMOs should be the creation of its mission, its value for its diverse stakeholders, and its vision for the future.

Strategic planners universally conclude that your first step in the destination marketing organization (DMO) planning and development process is review and development of your mission statement by the governing body.

Your mission statement should serve as the mirror for your organization, reflecting the clear reason for the existence of your DMO—why you are in business. And all future business planning and developments that follow must subscribe to it as the foundation of purpose. Therefore, it is critical that there be clarity and consensus around the mission.

What should it contain, and how should it be structured?

- It should be brief, no more than a sentence or two, so that it can be easily stated, remembered, and understood. It should focus solely on what the organization is—and the fundamental goal it is designed to achieve. The market segments and the marketing process to be deployed should be described in the marketing plan, but not included as part of this mission statement.
- It should be market-driven and responsible for achieving higher or incremental volumes of business for your community. But be mindful that if you are going to actually confirm your role in this regard, you should be prepared to produce quantifiable performance impacts in firm numbers and later forecast them for future delivery as part of a traditional marketing and business plan. This, after all, is what destination marketing is all about.

Here are other component thoughts for inclusion in your mission statement:

- Are you the community's official DMO?
- Do you fulfill the inclusionary needs of a public/private partnership?
- Do you produce positive results for residents as well as services for visitors?

In addressing the various requirements and needs listed by the board, a new mission statement, could read as follows:

We are the official tourism destination marketing organization for our community, committed to a public and private partnership to produce higher volumes of meetings, conventions, and leisure travel, and the resulting positive impacts of new visitor receipts and other benefits that support the region's economic prosperity.

Now that the mission statement is completed, it should be recognized and understood by all who are affiliated with the DMO. It is, in essence, your pledge of allegiance and your commitment to stakeholders. As such, it should be publicly reproduced and prominently displayed in your offices, incorporated in your annual marketing plan and other internal documents including annual reports—perhaps even on business-oriented press releases—and revisited as part of your strategic planning process.

Supporting Objectives

After production of the mission statement, you should clarify the important primary objectives that flow from it. Most DMOs fulfill six fundamental objectives:

- **Generate positive awareness** of the area as a destination of choice for meetings, conventions, and leisure travel business.
- **Stimulate interest and desire** on the part of consumers to take action and visit.
- **Increase the business volume** of the area's tourism business stakeholders and community constituents.
- **Proactively support the development** of additional tourism products and services to enhance the visitor experience.
- **Maintain a research base** for the community's tourism industry.
- **Create positive awareness, support, and participation** in the DMO and its marketing programs.

These broad-based objectives should fulfill the entire scope of work of the DMO. So for future recommended programs to be considered for inclusion, they should fit within the parameters of these objectives.

Clarifying the DMO's Value

Next, let's review what you actually produce on behalf of your community, and the tourism industry it serves, through the mission statement that you've just created.

Keep in mind that when your tourism economy is strong, as measured by tourism industry indicators, such as hotel occupancy, airport arrivals, and attractions attendance, those are certainly not the effective measurement of the

DMO's efforts—any more than a weak tourism market should conclude that your performance efforts are unsatisfactory.

Your organization is certainly not responsible for delivering the total and substantial economic benefits of community tourism. Yet some communities still infer that credit by stating the total community economic tourism impact immediately following their mission statements—and still in several isolated instances, DMOs continue to extrapolate data to overestimate their contributions. At least one such organization still divides its community's tax receipts by its annual operating budget to inaccurately conclude that for the dollars it expends for marketing, it is responsible for producing the entire community's resulting visitor tax revenue dollars. This kind of faulty logic impugns the reliability and integrity of DMO success.

Instead, quantitative performance productivity returns produced by your specific ongoing marketing programs are required. This includes all achievements that can be accurately and quantifiably measured. In most cases, that will include annual results achieved from such marketing programs as

- meeting and convention bookings
- group leisure bookings
- leisure visits produced from advertising, web development, etc.
- media destination story placement.

Productive dollar value returns from these performance categories will help answer the question: What is the value of the work of the DMO in fulfilling its mission?

You should begin by totaling up the estimated dollar results of annual productivity achieved and then crafting this new value statement for your organization. It might read as follows:

Last year, operating with a marketing staff of _____ and a $_____ marketing budget, the _____ DMO produced an estimated $_____ in new visitor dollars to the community, including _____ overnight leisure visitors and conference delegates.

In addition, staff-generated media publicity valued at more than $_____ reached ____ potential visitors (expressed in circulation/readership) who are now considering our destination for future visits.

Thus, on behalf of the City/County of _____ and its _____ business partners/members, the DMO delivered a ____-to-1 return-on-investment (divide the return by the annual DMO budget) of marketing dollars expended.

It is not unreasonable for you to produce between a 5-to-1 and a 30-to-1 return-on-investment (ROI) for your organization. Can you think of any business enterprise that comes close to consistently producing that kind of return? I can't, and neither can your stakeholders.

This value statement provides a very powerful response to the organization's mission statement. Although it only includes the tip of the iceberg in marketing value to the community, and doesn't address many other important aspects of your qualitative achievements including branding, business partnerships, and the like, it does clarify quantifiable dollar performance accountability and major annual ROI for all stakeholders.

You will find a number of ROI recommendations offered in the Destination Marketing Association International's Standard CVB Reporting Handbook. However, I believe this simple annual value statement provides the most useful ROI summary analysis for ongoing reporting.

The value statement should be most often prominently communicated immediately following the mission statement and in response to it in all appropriate DMO publications including the annual report, the annual marketing plan, business plans, and ongoing stakeholder reports. For future reference and comparison, one of the industry's most comprehensive models for effective ROI has been developed by Visit Baltimore.

Communicating Value for the DMO and the Destination: Two Best Practices

1. The Greater Miami CVB Industry Newsletter

"We're in the good news business," said Bill Talbert, president and CEO of the Greater Miami CVB; and you'll quickly agree with him when you read their newsletter, "What's Happening This Week."

It's easy to understand why Miami CVB management touts this weekly email reporting tool as one of its most successful communications initiatives. CVB members and other principal stakeholders receive it each Monday.

No fluff or frills—just clear, concise information that builds partnerships, consensus marketing, community understanding, good will, and support.

It follows a simple memo format that requires little reading time but packs a lot in reviewing staff work, recent industry accomplishments, and comarketing opportunities.

Highlighted sections include

- CVB and partner-produced leads for convention business
- trade show participation and results

- D.C. regional office happenings
- advertising, media publicity, and other marketing program results
- a save-the-date column for upcoming marketing meetings and membership opportunities
- a listing of upcoming meetings and conventions as well as business booked.

Request a copy by emailing Bill Talbert at talbert@gmcvb.com.

2. The Visit Baltimore 'About Us' Informational Flyer
It only takes a moment to digest this one-page summary about Baltimore's tourism industry, but you can't help being impressed by the substantial benefits provided by both the industry and the DMO that supports it.

Detailed performance result information is provided in these six brief sections:

- **Why Tourism Is a Good Investment:** Reviews the thousands of jobs in Maryland that are directly supported by tourism spending, along with taxes paid by visitors that save Maryland households additional taxation each year. Sources: Maryland Office of Tourism Development and Tourism Economics
- **Baltimore Travel:** Provides annual visitor numbers by segments, lengths of stay, and spending totals. Sources: Longwoods Travel USA and Tourism Economics
- **Visit Baltimore Performance:** Reviews information used to produce the value statement, including sales bookings, media publicity produced, visitors welcomed at the center, web development success, and total quantifiable economic dollar returns from these combined annual initiatives.
- **Maryland Travel:** Compares the total number of annual visitors to Maryland for the previous year and the billions of dollars in economic activity from the state's hotels, restaurants, and attractions. Sources: D. K. Shifflet & Associates Ltd. and the Maryland Office of Tourism Development
- **Visit Baltimore's Convention Center Impact:** Provides information in hosted events, event length of stay, number of attendees, local jobs supported by spending, and the center's generation of millions of dollars in state and local taxes. Source: Crossroads Consulting Services

- **Visit Baltimore Hotel Impact** (excluding convention center): Provides the number of non-center-related events, average length of stay, number of attendees, economic impact derived including state and local taxes and jobs generated and sustained. Source: Crossroads Consulting Services

For a copy of Visit Baltimore's "Ask Us," contact Jeff Hungate, chief operating officer, at jhungate@baltimore.org.

Developing a Vision for the DMO of the Future

What will your DMO be like in the future, and what values must you and your leadership embrace to make this become a reality?

These questions and process are usually a major step initiated for strategic plan development or as part of a board retreat exercise. But whenever it is implemented, it involves leadership input from members of the policy-making board. A facilitator-led exercise is undertaken for development of this new vision statement. Its objective: to chart a long-range successful course of the DMO in the fulfillment of its mission.

Participants are asked to take a few minutes to set aside the present and envision what the future DMO will resemble, thinking about it in this way:

It is five years from today's date, and we have created the area's optimum DMO. How do we describe it? And what values did we foster and embrace to create it? What do we value, and what would we like to see improved?

What will be included? Candor? Transparency? Ethics? Best business practices that guide the delivery of effective performance results? Strong partnership participation that leverages resources?

Board members are then asked to discuss and describe their aspirations for the new DMO. As they share their viewpoints, the facilitator memorializes the discussion and incorporates future requirements into a vision statement designed to guide the organization as it charts its future course.

Developing the CVB Vision Statement

During the visioning process for the Charlottesville Albemarle, VA CVB, board members listed their perceived attributes for the future CVB:

- a forward-looking board that embraces a productive strategic vision
- a well-trained, dedicated, and skilled staff

- a marketing program effort that consistently produces new and more business results for all
- an operation with candor, transparency, and best business principles in a full partnership with government and community business interests
- programs of performance and operational excellence to meet and exceed the professional standards of today's optimum DMO
- the community's respected leader for tourism development
- strong partnership support and marketing participation of community stakeholders and organizations
- a competitively funded program providing required manpower and marketing resources to achieve success.

The required attributes compiled by the board were then combined and incorporated to describe the vision of the emerging Charlottesville Albemarle CVB.

The Charlottesville Albemarle CVB Vision Statement

With strategic vision from the Board of Directors, performance excellence and innovation from the staff, productive positive stakeholder partnerships that inspire, involve, and support our travel community, and a competitive destination marketing program, we will continue to emulate and exceed the industry's highest professional standards and best business practices in a spirit of leadership, candor, and effective communications, delivering enhanced sales and service excellence for our clients and customers, as we strive to achieve the greatest performance success results for the city and county, and all of our residents.

This vision statement provides a strong and positive commitment for the future. Like the mission statement, it should be prominently posted at the DMO offices while also featured in marketing and annual planning documents.

The vision statement should be revisited as part of the organization's long-range strategic planning process for ongoing possible refinement and updating.

Creating Memorable Destinations: Positioning, Theming, and Branding

Isn't it terrific that the tourism industry has the magical ability to create memories that can last a lifetime?

I don't think anyone has ever captured that thought as eloquently as Pat Conroy, author of *The Prince of Tides*, who said, "Once you've traveled, the voyage never ends, but is played out over and over again in the quietest chambers . . . that the mind can never break off from the journey."

And that's really at the core of the destination CEO's job description: working to create a memorable destination of choice for visitors.

Although tourism marketing is comprised of many components and strategic initiatives—consumer research, product development, promotion, publicity, direct sales, advertising, website and Internet development, etc.—the most successful destination marketing innovators will be those who employ the processes of destination product positioning, theme development, and branding.

What Is Destination Product Positioning?

Positioning is the process of clarifying your community's principal visitor benefits, which positively separate your destination from other travel choices.

While there's only one London, Paris, and New York, your destination has motivational appeals that are capable of attracting specific customer groups.

For example:

- For Atlantic City, the positioning statement for the general consumer market once explained that for adult casino fun, A.C. was the most popular US visitor site with more than 37 million trips taken there annually. Thus, to deliver this attribute of popularity, this theme line was launched: "Atlantic City. America's Favorite Playground."
- For New York City, the positioning statement captured the principal appeals of world-renowned Broadway, other superlative entertainment, museums, shopping, dining, and sightseeing all wrapped in the excitement of the tourism industry's most exciting city. The resulting theme line: "New York. The World Capital of Excitement."

What are attributes of strategically produced winning campaigns?

Be unique. Destination appeals, dependent on their strengths, may be referred to as unique selling propositions. And if you define and prioritize them properly, imbuing them with sensory descriptions that put the consumer right in the middle of it all, you'll go a long way toward truly being unique in strategically positioning your visitor product in relation to the competition.

Lead with your strengths. It's also important to mention new products, facilities, amenities, or services, but always lead with your best foot forward through your principal strengths. Otherwise, you'll be diluting your communications message. So always highlight the benefits that mean the most to the largest potential universe of customers.

Listen to the customer. The customer is always right and should be listened to faithfully to keep your marketing efforts on track. While a snappy new theme line and zesty creative messages may sound great to you, they won't mean a thing if they don't address the consumers' inherent needs. And you'll only know if they're truly motivational by finding the answers through research that identifies the customers' attitudes, interests, and desires.

Stress convenience. Of course, not every destination can be unique. If you don't have the required attributes, then you can be convenient, by stressing your close-by location availability. One memorable convenience campaign produced by South Carolina embraced the theme, "Another day of sunshine." It conveyed the appealing message that if you lived in the Northeast and planned to drive south to Florida for vacation, you'd save time off the road and enhance your trip by staying in South Carolina instead.

Use compelling testimonials. Don't overlook opportunities for testimonial comments to position your visitor product. They may come from celebrity personalities who grew up in your community: sports figures, musicians, actors. Just be careful that potential consumers are favorably predisposed to these personalities or you may adversely generate apathy or ill will for your venue.

Let travel industry authorities do the talking for you. Publicize positive, credible comments about your area that have been made by nationally recognized meeting planners for the convention marketplace and by travel writers / consumer publications for the leisure travel market. Major attributable sources such as national travel magazines, trade publications, and nationally recognized newspapers have great cache and solid reputations with the consumer that you should want to incorporate in your message delivery.

Prepare for the long-term usage of a winning campaign. Changing a campaign without compelling reasons will destroy any equity it has generated in relationship to other competing campaigns that continue to inform potential customers about their ongoing benefits.

The Destination Positioning and Theme Development Processes

Today's most successful tourism programs are supported by persuasive motivational messages that comprise a destination's product positioning statement.

That positioning is then used to guide the development of the tourism destination's theme line. Properly developed and executed positioning statements and resultant destination theme lines have been consistently shown to measurably contribute to generating higher volumes of positive destination public awareness, consumer interest, and intent to visit.

The best industry marketing processes for destination positioning and theme development follow:

Step 1. Benefit Testing Analysis: For the initial step, key staff and other community communications constituents are called upon to produce up to seven broad-based destination appeals that offer a variety of priority messages capable of motivating visitors from all leisure market segments. These appeals may be based on written and visual inputs, including major attractions, community attributes, icons, and sensory experiences and may include

- historical attractions
- cultural appeals such as performing arts
- family fun
- outdoor recreation
- the destination's proximity to other amenities
- convenient location
- its cost/value relationship.

The final selection of the preferred destination benefit description is then made by potential consumers through research analysis. Some marketers employ customer focus groups (both for the visitor and the nonvisitor segments). At least two focus groups would usually be conducted, and geographic locations, along with invitees' consumer profiles, would be determined and approved. However, my preferred methodology for benefit testing and selection is through Internet-based research that is both cost efficient and projectable to the total universe of visitors to the destination. This process assures that the DMO gathers actionable data and not just directional opinions.

Step 2. The Destination Product Positioning Statement: Once the most effective broad-based destination appeal is chosen based on consumer preferences, it should be crafted and communicated in a narrative paragraph that provides the most effective statement that separates the destination from other competitors. Whenever feasible, this positioning should incorporate "big name" descriptors and not just generic destination appeals. This positioning statement becomes the priority marketing message for the DMO that consistently describes and introduces the destination on its website, in collateral and for other supportive communications media and messages.

Step 3. Theme Line Development: Next comes the creation of the new theme line that flows from the positioning statement, usually by creating four or five theme choices, which again are selected and prioritized through consumer research. They should be tested against these four important attributes:

- It is a credible description of the destination.
- It makes the destination seem appealing.
- It suggests a positive sense of the community.
- It makes the consumer more willing to consider the destination for visitation.

Your objective is to measure believability, appeal, uniqueness, and motivation, along with any meaningful negatives that might be present. Importantly, the selection of your destination theme line should not be viewed as a popularity contest.

The final theme recommendation should be chosen that best fulfills these measurement criteria and sets the destination apart for the long term. Uniqueness, without negatives, should be your desired goal.

Step 4. A Graphic Logo Incorporating the Theme: Ultimately, this initiative should guide development of the DMO's array of collateral communications programs including direct mail, advertising, website positioning, media publicity programs, exhibits, and signage. The development of the graphic logo or mark should include testing and usage online where many first impressions will take place, because a logo that works on paper sometimes does not resonate online.

However, for this program to prove successful, it must also enjoy the proactive participation and exponential use from the destination's constituents in their own marketing communications delivery systems. A usage manual should be produced by the graphics/ad agency. Logo art sheets are recommended in one approved format, but in several sizes and colors, including in multiple colors, in black and white, and in reverse.

Step 5. Theme Launching: A staff-driven plan for a public roll-out of the theme line should be produced. This celebratory meeting should have as its principal purpose the agreement by stakeholders to get on-board in their own use of the theme line/logo—for their own collateral, in ads, media publicity, and sales efforts. An ongoing community culturization plan should follow.

Keep in mind that logos and theme lines aren't brands. They are merely representations of brands. They are the entry point and the shortcut to the brand for your mind. Brands are not concrete; they are the thoughts, feelings, and psychological relationships between a business and a customer. And your brand is the foundation of all your marketing activities.

The Destination Branding Process

You may recall iconic American writer, poet, and art collector Gertrude Stein's telling remark when she was asked about her childhood home of Oakland, California. "Oakland?" she responded. "There's no 'there,' there." She could have been referring to the need for destination branding.

The American Marketing Association defines a brand as a "name, term, design, symbol, or any other feature that identifies one seller's good or service as distinct from those of other sellers. The legal term for *brand* is *trademark*. A brand may identify one item, a family of items, or all items of that seller. If used for the firm as a whole, the preferred term is *trade name*."

That definition of a brand is certainly narrow.

What Is a Destination Brand?

In destination tourism marketing, *branding* or *brand identity* is

The total sum of the words, images, and associations that form the customer's perception of the destination.

The brand, therefore, is the conveyed personality of the visitor's experience.

If you want to maximize your destination's opportunities for success, you must address the need for a branding process, because if a brand is simply a promise, link, or bridge between the customer and your travel destination, then you already have a brand. But what it currently conveys to your customers is another story.

A brand is the collective relationships that you foster with customers that will create brand equity over time. Brand equity is the value of your marketing organization or your visitor product—far beyond its physical attributes. And you should want your positive destination brand to live in the hearts and heads of customers.

Your destination's brand must also permeate your entire community, and is not based on individual attractions, amenities, and services, but on the collective visitor product. This must include the product's reputation as well, the people who serve visitors, the programs you produce, and the look and feel of all you do and say. Yes, branding should truly be everybody's job.

Qualities for Successful Brand Development

Here are the seven qualities of a successful brand initiative, according to the industry book, *Destination BrandScience*.

    1. Front-load total buy-in. From the outset, leadership and key stakeholders have to believe wholeheartedly and enthusiastically in the approach, or the destination brand will fall short of its anticipated goals.

2. It is not about advertising; your brand is a strategic asset. To become a distinctive, one-of-a-kind destination brand that wins the hearts and minds of visitors requires an integrated strategic approach to brand development. Brands are more than names, symbols, or slogans. A genuine brand is the "internalized sum of all impressions received by visitors and prospective visitors, resulting in a distinctive position in their 'mind's eye' based on perceived emotional and functional behavior." Advertising and promotion are important, but only after a distinctive promise is developed. Remember, from the visitor's perspective, a destination brand is all about the experience.

3. Adhere to a set of principles. Establish a set of brand values and principles to guide behavior and decision making.

4. Stand out to stand apart. The destination brand platform must be built on a set of attributes and factors that distinguish it from competitors in the minds and perspectives of visitors, influencers, and stakeholders.

5. Brand evangelists are critical. To ensure total commitment and support at the most important levels of government, everyone throughout the community from the very top to the very bottom becomes an evangelist for the brand. No one person alone can champion the cause. It takes the team to ensure that all messages are aligned with the promise.

6. Consistency, consistency, consistency. Staying true to the road map by following the designated course of action and messages is the path to attaining destination brand goals.

7. Live the promise. A genuine destination brand is a pact with visitors. Successful brands keep their commitments with visitors and enthusiastically deliver on the promise throughout the entire community.

We are familiar with a number of brand development programs; some are more successful than others. Getting there requires a disciplined process, of which there are several in vogue today.

The Preferred Model for Destination Brand Development

Our favored process is produced by Believable Brands' Gary Sherwin, based on the book *Destination BrandScience*, which he coauthored. The brief descriptive outline includes the following:

Step 1. Brand Analysis and Research: Formal brand research of visitors/nonvisitors and stakeholder interviews. Review of existing Brand position and execution of community wide Brand Summit.

Step 2. Brand Benchmark: Review of research data to determinate key destination attributes and emotional connections among visitors and stakeholders.

Step 3. Brand Promise: A clear definition and description of the destination's emotional and functional benefits that will serve as the "Guiding Star" for all future brand development and marketing efforts.

Step 4. Brand Enrichment: Creation of the specific steps necessary to bring the destination brand to life. This will include working with the ad agency on logo and tagline development as well as recommending possible service training programs or infrastructure development.

Step 5. Brand Future: Suggestion of strategic partnerships that can leverage the destination brand among the community and grow its brand equity.

Step 6. Brand Blueprint: Development of a formal working document that highlights all of the activities described above and will serve as the reference tool for all community presentations and for staff referral.

Gary Sherwin can be reached at gary@believablebrands.com.

The Virginia Is for Lovers Story

Four decades ago, Virginia launched the Virginia Is for Lovers Campaign—what is now arguably the first and most successful destination brand-positioning state tourism program. Here's the fascinating story of how it was developed, its significant influence on other destination marketing programs, and a few lessons learned.

Take it from someone who was there. Virginia Is for Lovers was not only the groundbreaking, nationally award-winning, and wildly successful state tourism development program that is still going strong today (Forbes.com recently named it one of the top ten tourism marketing campaigns of all time), it was also a major accidental occurrence and a stroke of great luck.

How did it actually happen? What did it really come to mean? And what did the campaign achieve for Virginia's tourism industry?

Back In the Day

Let's take a quick trip back to the late 1960s when new social winds were beginning to blow across the United States, issuing a clarion call for universal love and happiness.

In 1967, the "American tribal love rock musical *Hair*" premiered on Broadway. Popular song lyrics from the Mamas and the Papas urged hippie adventurers on their way to San Francisco to "be sure to wear some flowers in your hair." Two years later, in 1969, the year's best new musical artists Crosby, Stills, Nash, and Young introduced the mantra, "Carry on . . . Love is coming . . . Love is coming to us all." This was also the year of Woodstock, the era of free love and communal love-ins. (And make no mistake about it; sexual connotations were the constant subliminal messages.)

The Viet Nam war was raging while young people demonstrated in the streets, proclaiming, "Make love, not war."

Author Erich Segal hit it big with his best seller, *Love Story*, and the popular movie that followed. It's little wonder that this period quickly became known as the Love Generation.

You can begin to see why the word *love* was considered all the rage and predestined to soon burst upon the scene of America's tourism industry.

A New Tourism Campaign for Virginia

It was during this period that Virginia's tourism advertising contract was about to expire. A request was issued for advertising agency proposals and a new campaign to attract the leisure market. I was also about to be named Virginia's newest and youngest commissioner for tourism.

One of the firms pitching the advertising account was a group of talented young people headed by David Martin, its president who also had a creative bent, and Vice President George Woltz, who despite his senior creative role at the agency also had solid business acumen. Together, the team at Martin and Woltz began preparing a new marketing approach that, if selected, would provide a major departure from the current state tourism campaign.

As a first step, the M&W team wisely concluded that the state's visitor market was static. Earlier that year, a new visitor profile study had estimated that while Virginia's travel market was better educated and more affluent than regional competitors, it was also an aging demographic. And while the good news showed that visitors to Virginia kept returning often—one out of three had been there up to seven times—the younger adult market with the greatest long-term potential for future visitation was not being courted through state advertising.

Why should we continue to focus on the older traditional visitor who already had such destination loyalty for Virginia, the Martin and Woltz firm questioned. Instead, the agency team envisioned an opportunity to win new minds by mirroring many of the interests and lifestyle attributes of the emerging young adult market having children, and who would soon become the mainstay of Virginia's travel market.

The state's current tourism campaign, The Faces of Virginia, with its stoic, old-fashioned black-and-white photos of attractions and scenery, was considered by many to be staid, passive, and dull.

Catching the New Wave of Social Change

What was needed, the M&W agency believed, was a communications approach that evoked the current milieu: cool, hip, cutting edge, and in synch with the social change that was sweeping the country.

The M&W agency's proposed campaign featured the vibrancy of full-color photography that captured the excitement of young families rollicking in the ocean, trekking along the Blue Ridge Mountains, and stepping back in time at Colonial Williamsburg, Jamestown, and Yorktown. There were also seasonal approaches targeted to the couples market such as upscale fall visitation opportunities and romantic winter getaways.

Introducing the Lovers Concept

But the most innovative step was when the agency decided to introduce and then weave the socially popular theme of love throughout its creative approach. In the ad featuring historical attractions, for example, the headline read, "Virginia Is for *History* Lovers." For the beach ad's headline, "Virginia Is for *Beach* Lovers."

Shortly before the campaign presentation was readied for the state, a junior ad agency creative department staffer offered this thought: "Why don't we just take out the history and beaches and other appeals. Instead, let it just be, 'Virginia Is for Lovers.'" Everyone at the agency quickly embraced the idea and what it came to mean: no matter what you loved—history, beaches, mountains, or the like—you'd find it all in Virginia.

It may not seem so cutting edge today, but in the late 1960s it was borderline risqué and provocative for a government tourism agency to introduce a lovers theme into the lexicon of tourism marketing.

When the new campaign was officially presented to the decision-making body of the Virginia Department of Conservation and Economic Development that oversaw state tourism, one of its conservative, gray-haired board members responded enthusiastically. "I don't think any of us are too old not to be considered a Virginia Lover, and I recommend approval." And so the board unanimously did just that without a blink.

At first, the state didn't really know the significant value of what it had with this new campaign—not until it was introduced to clients at a national travel show. When the staff quickly ran out of lapel buttons featuring the white-lettered logo and bright red heart emblazoned across a shiny black background, one enthusiastic attendee responded, "I'll give you $25 for one of those buttons!" At that precise moment, we knew we had something quite special.

What followed was the comprehensive integration of the lovers theme through all marketing programs and media: collateral including the new full-color visitor guide and vertical publications including camping, skiing, and golf; public relations (PR) and media publicity; and sales programs and presentations for tour operators and other emerging market segments.

When the in-state public service campaign was launched to stimulate travel by Virginians, the TV spots featured Miss Virginia Debbie Shelton. As luck would have it, she soon went on to gain greater notoriety for the state campaign when she was selected as Miss USA several months later.

In one TV video, as Debbie and her companion were filmed romantically strolling along Virginia Beach, back-grounded by the ocean's lapping waves, the camera came in for a close-up of her "Virginia Is for Lovers" T-shirt. Almost immediately, a new cottage industry sprang up to produce a wide variety of lovers merchandise: shirts, pens, coasters, posters, glassware. Tens of thousands of bumper stickers were shipped to the state's highway visitor welcome centers and soon became provocative little traveling billboards for Virginia when they appeared on most out-of-state cars heading back home following family vacations.

Most importantly, the campaign was soon enthusiastically endorsed by Virginia's tourism industry business stakeholders.

What was really innovative was the way the campaign later unfolded and matured through so many creative nuances that continued to breathe new life in it for decades. Ads for autumn included this headline: "Fall. In Love. In Virginia." For the honeymoon market, this copy appeared: "Love is an eight-letter word. In a word, Virginia, because all the things you love are here."

Months later, the National Premium Association suggested to its membership that the current big deal was "the smiley face logo" and "(blank) ___ is for lovers"—"Just insert your city or state," it suggested. Unfortunately, a number of businesses did just that—and they were quickly followed with some terse phone calls from the Virginia Attorney General's office who had handled registration for the lovers logo and theme line.

If imitation is the sincerest form of flattery, the lovers campaign was certainly flattered to death. Entrants in quick succession included: "Alabama Is for Livers," "Missouri Loves Company," and "Maryland Is for Crabs." Then eight years later, in 1977, the "I Love New York" campaign was created.

In the early 1980s, a Virginia State Secretary of Commerce tried to gain traction with a replacement campaign, "Virginia. Exciting Times Every Time." But no one embraced the approach, and it was discarded with the quick reinstatement of the lovers theme as if it had never left.

What the Campaign Achieved

From Virginia's campaign inception, positive consumer awareness grew. So did corresponding interest in visiting Virginia. Despite its provocative nature, there were no measurable negative connotations.

In just three short years, the percentage of young adult families to Virginia grew from the low 20 percent to the mid-30 percent range. Top-of-mind interest in Virginia as a major destination by both tour operators and the media alike also consistently grew.

Here are a few things we learned over the years:

- With destination tourism themes, market positioning, and brand development, follow the golden rule: never change a winning game. To assure success, you must be prepared to stay the course and build positive awareness for the long term.
- Changing campaigns doesn't mean changing your brand. However, because some destination marketers work on and see their campaign every day, they sometimes not only change their campaigns too quickly but also develop campaigns that don't support their brand. It's an important lesson that changing a campaign has the potential of destroying the valuable brand equity that you have just begun to foster.

- However, being aware of changing marketing conditions and ways to breathe new life into ongoing campaigns can help maintain the brand equity while catering to new market demands.

Keep It Fresh

Virginia continues to keep the lovers campaign current, memorable, and targeted to today's consumer, thanks to the savvy and skilled staff at the Virginia Tourism Corporation.

"Based upon the brand equity we've achieved over the last forty years and the continued positive response from our target markets, we know that our brand is delivering on our promise of a great travel experience," said Alisa Bailey, president and CEO of Virginia Tourism Corporation. "We recently initiated the supportive line, 'Live Passionately,' which gives a renewed meaning to "Virginia Is for Lovers," allowing us to capitalize upon the consumers' growing interest in what has become known as experiential or enrichment travel."

Theme Lines, Not Tag Lines

If you develop a theme line that adequately serves to help pay off the promise of your destination's market positioning, refer to it as just that: a theme line, and never as a tag line.

A tag line sounds like nothing more than a passing fancy, one that has no permanence and is, therefore, of little worth, just tagging along, an undervalued appendage that can be easily discarded and replaced.

Don't Rely on Your Instincts

Remember that ongoing consumer research is a necessity in monitoring the recognition and positive value of your campaign in changing consumer attitudes, destination awareness, and interest to visit.

Was "Virginia Is for Lovers" in any way a model for today's tourism campaigns and brand development programs? Not really. After all, it was created more than forty years ago without the benefit of projectable consumer research or advanced pretesting techniques readily available today.

Yet while the lovers theme may have indeed been a lucky, accidental achievement, it was also somehow born to succeed—and that it has surely done in so many tangible, winning ways.

Going Forward, Be Thought Provoking

As you prepare to develop your next new campaign—after you've made sure it's on target with consumers based on your destination's motivational appeals—there's one other very important requirement: be aggressively thought provoking, delivering a creatively distinctive and memorable campaign that is different from anything else out there.

It is this "wow" factor that is found only in truly great destination campaign themes. You should reach for and accept nothing less.

It All Begins with the Customer

No matter how well funded and staffed your organization may be, to accomplish the mission, you must first fully understand your customers and their perceptions of the destination, because only they can unlock the information you need for fostering an effective marketing program.

To illustrate the importance of thoroughly listening to the customer, here's an anecdote from long-time tourism marketer John Boatright, who was handling the advertising account for Colonial Williamsburg. Consumers weren't responding to the old ads, CW officials said, primarily because about fifty of their older hotel rooms were outfitted with two single beds that couples didn't wish to select.

"Please design a campaign that'll motivate more couples to book these accommodations," Williamsburg officials requested. "How much money do you have for the campaign?" Boatright asked, and they estimated $50,000 was available for ad purchases. His response was immediate and truly customer focused: "You should just take that money and buy fifty queen-sized beds," he advised. "It'll take care of your problem this year as well as for years to come." The people at Williamsburg did just that and began seeing positive results from happy new couples.

Then there's the classic story about the architect who was asked to design a cobblestone walkway connecting a newly constructed building to the nearby feeder parking lot. But instead of immediately tackling the task by laying out the walkway grid, he instead planted grass seed on the bare patch of land that separated the parking area from the building. During the following months, people tramped across the grass to their cars, wearing a discernible pathway that best met their needs—and that became his design model. The architect simply followed their worn path, constructing it in stone—another testimony for the need to pay attention to the customer.

The Importance of Customer Perceptions

"Seriously," industry marketing expert John Boatright has always urged, "don't think about spending a dollar on programming until you've clarified your visitor markets and their potentials."

Clearly, research is the critical first step in defining your future needs including customer perceptions. Because understanding each customer's needs and motivations, and then providing the highest quality visitor product or service in response, should drive your ongoing business decision-making.

The recommended annual funding allocation for ongoing research to guide destination marketing programs should amount to between 2 and 5 percent of the organization's total budget.

For DMO consideration and future reference, here are the two major research programs produced by leading industry research firm Longwoods International:

1. Visitor Tracking Research

- visitor volumes and spending
- visitor demographics
- visitor activities

Longwoods International has been tracking travel in the United States since 1990. The Longwoods Travel USA® program is currently the largest ever ongoing survey of US leisure and business travel. Each quarter, a random cross-section of approximately 500,000 panelists is sent an e-mail invitation to participate in the survey, for a total outgo of 2 million contacts annually. Subscribers to Longwoods Travel USA® receive a detailed profile of visitors to their destination, including trip planning, transportation, accommodations, activities, expenditures, competitive position, and demographics. The cost of this massive program is shared by many Longwoods' clients, including countries, states, cities, regions, associations, and the private sector, thus providing them with excellent value in comparison to custom research. As subscribers to Longwoods Travel USA®, clients are allowed access to the complete database through ASTEROID™, a user-friendly analysis program. This allows them to conduct custom analyses, not only for trips to their destination, but for all destinations.

2. Image and Advertising Evaluation Research

- What are visitor and nonvisitor perceptions about you as a travel destination?
- How does the destination stack up against its key competitors?
- What is important to the potential visitor in selecting the destination?
- Is your advertising working to
  - improve your image as a travel destination?
  - motivate incremental travel to the destination and increased traveler spending?
- If the destination spends a dollar on marketing tourism, what does it get back in terms of new state and local tax dollars?

Image and advertising evaluation research is designed to profile awareness of the destination as a place to visit, its image strengths and weaknesses, and the factors important in the decision to visit the destination:
- Quantify and provide a credible measure of the effectiveness of the

destination's tourism advertising and its incremental impact on the destination's bottom line in terms of travel expenditures and taxes.
- Provide insight into how to optimize future yields through creative, media, and tactical enhancements.

Longwoods not only estimates the incremental impact of communications programs on sales, but also provides insight into how to optimize future yields through creative, media, and tactical enhancements. This research is conducted by an online panel among a statistically representative sample of US adults in the client's key advertising markets.

The **Benchmark** component of the survey questionnaire investigates

- key travel motivators
- the image of the destination across an extensive battery of 40+ characteristics, customized to include any unique client characteristics
- the image of up to six competitive destinations and their relative strengths and weaknesses
- the client's image versus product delivery as inferred from the image ratings of recent visitors
- interest in visiting client versus competitors.

The **Accountability/ROI** section of the survey determines

- awareness of client's advertising
- the impact of this awareness on client's image
- short-term conversion, e.g., trips taken as a direct result of client's advertising during and immediately following the campaign
- intentions to visit in the future.

For additional information, contact Dr. Bill Siegel, founder and chairman of Longwoods International at bsiegel@longwoods-intl.com.

Customer Surveys

A range of customer surveys, via the Internet, can help facilitate the quick and cost-effective capturing of essential data for understanding critical customer perceptions and needs. There are several priority customers that will require your attention:

- The leisure travel visitor market should be your first priority.
- Travel intermediaries work on your behalf to reach many of your targets, e.g., meeting planners, travel writers, and tour operators.

- Community local stakeholders, or internal customers, including government and business interests that partner with the DMO.

There are two priority customer needs to address in the customer surveys:

1. Reaching and Understanding the Leisure Market

Traditional visitor profile studies may provide all the information you need for both building a foundation of customer understanding and addressing a marketing plan of engagement.

I favor an analysis of both the visitor and the nonvisitor to your destination. And if your destination is like most other destinations that are primarily frequented by relatively close-in overnight drive markets—say within a 300- to 400-mile radius that may contribute about 80 percent of your visitors—that is where you should throw the net for analysis. About 600 survey respondents can produce a study that is projectable to your universe of potential visitors.

The sample for the Internet survey can be procured by analysts through a national survey panel with millions of consumers that match US census data within 1 percent and are representative of the larger North American population. What's more, panel members have previously completed an extensive personal profile that goes well beyond the normal demographics of age, gender, location, income, etc. As a result, the research firm should be able to select survey participants according to more than 120 lifestyle characteristics, including travel interests and behaviors. Respondents to your survey should be recruited according to the following criteria:

- males and females living within a required geographic area
- people having taken a leisure trip and stayed in a hotel within the past twelve months
- people involved in planning vacations or leisure trips for the household
- people with $50,000+ annual household income.

When hiring a firm, be sure to look not only at its Internet-based work for other destinations and its ability to tailor a program to your needs, but also its expertise for top brands and institutions, such as major attractions, airlines, major hotel chains, and resorts.

Your online survey instrument should be designed to assess various aspects of the leisure travel market for your destination. Also, as part of a broader effort to further define potential visitors, evaluate current marketing activities, clarify area attribute/amenity appeals, and enhance messaging, the survey should address these key areas:
- **developing a detailed picture** of the current and potential visitor market in terms of demographics, attitudes, travel needs, and behaviors

- **understanding what nonvisitors are looking for** in vacation destinations and how to best attract them to visit your destination in the future
- **evaluating the importance of attributes** and amenities that drive visitation
- **measuring awareness, familiarity, visitation, and consideration** of the area relative to nearby destinations
- **measuring perceptions of your visitor attributes** in the context of competitive destinations and key drivers of visitation
- **identifying new facilities and services** that would attract more visitors
- **understanding how current communications are working** and uncovering potential ways to improve your future messaging
- **measuring visit satisfaction**, likes/dislikes/wish lists, and likelihood to recommend.

Survey costs are in the $20,000 range. The leading firm with whom we often work for production of these tailored studies is EquationResearch.com. Contact John Pelletier, chairman, at jpelletier@equationresearch.com.

2. Addressing Travel Intermediary Opinions and Needs

Next, I recommend development of surveys for meeting planners, tour operators, travel writers, and DMO stakeholders. Produced at least every three years, the objectives of these surveys are to

- identify problems to improve service quality or supporting systems, processes, and procedures
- establish benchmarks and measure progress going forward
- enable customers or stakeholders to freely express their opinions about the quality of service provided
- send a positive message to customers/stakeholders that their business is valued and the focus is on continuous improvement to meet their needs.

The Meeting Planner Survey: Meeting planners who now produce meetings for the destination would be asked to rate the following categories:

- quality of the convention center facility
- quality of hotel facilities
- management of convention/meeting requirements
- quality of hotel accommodations
- quality of food and beverage
- quality of planning and administration for both the convention sales and convention services departments
- quality of customer service from the convention sales and convention services departments.

Meeting planners should be asked their overall opinion on what the DMO did really well. They should also be asked to comment on anything they were unhappy about and to make suggestions to improve convention processes or quality of customer service.

The Tour Operator Survey: Tour operator surveys would be directed to those who bring group tours to the destination. The focus is on perceptions of the destination as an attraction and the quality of service provided by the tourism staff.

Tour operators would be asked to indicate multiple characteristics of their business in relationship to the destination. They would be asked to rate the following categories:

- quality of accommodations
- quality of attractions
- quality of restaurants
- experience at destination
- quality of DMO's promotional activities and services.

The tour operators should also be asked what the DMO did really well, to comment on anything they were unhappy about, and for suggestions to improve the quality of the DMO's customer service.

The focus of the survey is on very specific aspects of customer service, with the opportunity for narrative comments and responses to open-ended questions.

This is very effective for zeroing in on specific areas for improvement. Typical categories are as follows:

- quality of product, service, or program
- quality of customer service from staff
- professionalism and competence
- other operational aspects for review and feedback.

The Travel Writer Survey: The third survey instrument would target travel writers who both have visited and who have not visited the destination. The emphasis is on travel knowledge and destination product, along with staff service skills in accommodating writers.

Writers would be asked to indicate multiple characteristics of their business in relationship to the destination. They would then be prompted to rate the following categories:

- quality and interest level of attractions
- quality of restaurants, hotels, and other facilities
- experience at destination

- quality of DMOs service and support
- quality of DMOs promotional activities and services
- quality of product, service, or program
- quality of customer service from staff
- staff professionalism and competence.

The writers would then be asked for what the DMO did really well, to comment on anything they were unhappy about, for suggestions to improve the quality of the DMOs customer service, and other operational aspects for review and feedback.

Total costs for producing all three surveys should be in the $10,000 range.

The DMO Stakeholder Assessment Survey: It's always beneficial to determine ongoing stakeholder input regarding the DMO and how well it fulfills the needs of its partners.

The optimal method for assessing DMO stakeholder levels of support and need is through a third-party online survey that provides anonymity. It offers the most accurate method of gaining participant input and guidance. Questions for this assessment are based on traditional programs and services of today's DMO and can be edited as required.

In most cases, the survey should be provided to all stakeholders over the name of the organization's chairman with the resulting confidential responses by stakeholders returned directly to the firm that conducts the survey.

Responses should be segmented and provided by several areas, including resorts, hotels, attractions, government officials, the DMO board, restaurants, culture and arts, and others you deem appropriate for your analysis.

Questions are given a rating between one and five for each question and resulting categories.

Five major categories should be rated by participants, which include detailed questions that address how well the organization is performing in relationship to

- fulfilling the DMO's mission
- promoting the destination through various strategic and tactical initiatives
- quality customer service
- community outreach and awareness
- organizational leadership for visitor-related economic development.

Costs for the stakeholder assessment survey should be in the $4,000 range.

The industry leader in development of these customer and stakeholder assessments is Performance Solutions. Contact President Wil Brewer at wbrewer@ performance-solutions-group.com.

A Stakeholder Assessment Case Study

When the president of an emerging regional tourism organization decided to resign, instead of the board responding by seeking a qualified replacement, they appointed his secretary to fill the position. And so began the encroaching role of board members in staff micromanagement, assuming the role for creative direction for what is normally staff-developed work including advertising and collateral publications, while distancing themselves from the growing policy needs and concerns of the membership at large.

A newly formed independent strategic planning committee urged that a stakeholder assessment be produced to take a barometer of the membership—where the organization was going and how it should get there. The board agreed, but publicly expressed doubts that anyone would have disagreements with them about the organization's direction or leadership.

The results were dramatic and alarming to the board:

- Rank-and-file members disagreed with current management direction and called for an immediate restructuring of the board with new designated seat representation and term limits.
- They also overwhelmingly endorsed a new strategic plan.
- To the board's credit, it began to work with the membership and the strategic planning committee to chart a new and exciting direction for the DMO.
- As a result, the organization's budget and community support more than tripled within the next three years, reaching a much broader visitor market and producing increased business for their 700 members.

The Emerging Trend of Experiential Travel

"Today is Tuesday," said the peripatetic traveler to his wife, "We must be in Rome." That was the characteristic approach during an earlier era when fashionably sophisticated travelers collected destinations on their world travels. Then came new generations of travelers who began creating destination memories. Today, a new era of experiential travel is emerging that is actually transforming the consumer—and creating new destination marketing opportunities everywhere.

There's a new paradigm on the horizon for leisure travel today. Increasingly, the twenty-first-century traveler is seeking out trips that provide new, valuable experiences that raise their consciousness, develop new skills, and actually change their lives.

The US Travel Association has labeled it *enrichment travel*—others refer to it as *immersion* or *experiential* travel—and confirm that there's a trend on the rise with these recent research findings:

- More than half of visitors recently polled expressed interest in taking an educational trip, and nearly a quarter said they were more interested in this than they were five years ago.
- The quarterly Longwoods Travel USA survey concludes that over four out of ten American vacationers are now confirming the "experience travel" choices, according to Dr. Bill Siegel, CEO and founder of Longwoods International.

Travel Marketers Are Responding

The travel industry is beginning to respond to this growing trend in a number of ways. Some are attempting to repackage and reposition the traditional pastime of sightseeing and attractions-hopping based on consumer interests. Other destinations are now marketing new visitor product opportunities for their target audiences.

A major marketing thrust has recently been developed by the Canadian Tourism Commission (CTC). "Experiential tourism," said CTC CEO Michele McKenzie, "is fundamental to bringing our tourism brand to life to entice international travelers to Canada." In October 2011, according to McKenzie, the Commission announced the latest qualifying members in a collection that showcases brand-aligned Canadian tourism experiences from coast to coast. This brings to date 115 unique experiences ready to market to high-spending international travelers.

Tour operators have also taken note. "We're evolving and developing product to meet the demands of a brand new market of seasoned, educated, well-heeled travelers who demand and desire more than stopping, standing and staring," said Randy Julian, former chair of the National Tourism Association.

Examples of these experiential offerings include ethnic cooking in Mexico, hiking from a Waldenesque pond during New England's fall foliage season, teaching teens about the fashion industry in New York City, culinary academy classes, wine tasting excursions, and craft making. Then there are new twists on social tourism, including helping locals through programs such as Habitat for Humanity. But it doesn't end there. It can also provide new ways of seeing and experiencing communal travel opportunities with friends and relatives that bring participants closer together through shared time and experiences.

Noted travel writer and world traveler Pam Grout has called these trips "before and after" vacations "because, after one of them, you're probably going to be a little bit different," she said.

The Destination Market Potential Is Deep

This new trend of enrichment travel affords excellent opportunities for so many communities that feature special places for individual renewal—where visitors can experience something personal and lasting—and potentially life changing.

During a marketing assignment in South Dakota, I was personally drawn to the strong experiential appeals of the Black Hills, Badlands, and Lakes area, where, like many other regions, visitors can become explorers in surroundings that are exciting, enriching, and of superior value—through history, folklore, and local culture provided by those we meet.

No tour company or visitor product has marketed this concept quite as well as the Disney Corporation through its tour operator program.

"Live the Amazing Stories Behind the World's Greatest Destinations" was the headline offer in advertising spreads for Adventures by Disney. For North America, Disney has offered three vacation products: the Mid-Atlantic, the American Southwest, and Wyoming. Through its program, Disney said it was providing "a whole new way for families to travel together," that "Adventures by Disney vacations are unforgettable, immersive," and provide "travel experiences for families to explore the world's greatest destinations."

Fortunately, Adventures by Disney holds no monopoly on visitor destinations where special travel experiences are waiting to be discovered.

How to Embrace Experiential Travel

Making this strong, visceral connection with the consumer takes new and creative skills and a fresh look at your visitor appeals and offerings.

The technique calls for creating exciting descriptors and graphics that dramatically put the visitor right in the middle of the travel product—and convey strong sensory appeals that aren't often found in communications messages to travelers—yet sensory "hooks" were the strongest motivators when Colonial Williamsburg ran advertising that romanced the viewer with the stirring sights, aromas, and sounds of Duke of Gloucester Street, including delicious, freshly baked warm gingerbread enjoyed by children visiting the Governor's Mansion.

I'm also impressed with ads for the Pocono Mountains that invite travelers to "Discover, Exhale, Conquer and Explore." That says it all to outdoor travel enthusiasts. So does the Virginia Beach Tourism ad message, "Live the Life. Lose yourself. Find yourself."

Here are some other suggestions to consider for enhancing your marketing communications approaches:

- **Follow the recommendations from travelers** in new visitor profile studies that are most apt to bring visitor attention, interest, and desire.
- **Make it personal. Deliver fresh, powerful copy, and appeals** that emotionally engage the traveler and describe the destination such as, "Step back in time for historical adventures . . . majestic mountain discoveries . . . New journeys just around the corner . . . exploring the Spirit of America." As part of this approach, deliver the sensory experiences that best vividly describe your special sights, sounds, and conveyed feelings.
- **Use recognizable big names.** People in general are most attracted by specifics—not generalities. You should combine appeals and experiences provided in your destination with the well-known, identifiable names and sites—and share how personal experiences can be created in so many rewarding and fascinating ways. With most generic appeal tourism ads, if you cover up the name of the destination, you could be just about anywhere—and anywhere is not where you want to be, is it?
- **Employ larger dramatic photos** whenever feasible that include visitor adventurers who are shown experiencing the travel product. These larger photos will serve to anchor nearby smaller photos.
- **Incorporate graphic icons/art** of indigenous memorabilia throughout the collateral that connote the destination personality of the community.
- **Use testimonials to motivate visitors.** Third-party positive comments about your destination from both media and well-known public figures are far more credible to consumers than traditional promotional or advertising copy.

Here are a couple of great examples from the Black Hills:

- "An all-American road trip, filled with cowboys and Indians, buffalo

and prairie dogs, and dreamers. . . ." *San Diego Union-Tribune*
- "The Black Hills rises out of the Badlands, inviting exploration of rock spires, clear lakes, cool forests and main-street strolling towns." *Cottage Living Magazine*

Be Bold and Creative

Above all, keep up with the market direction that is consistently provided by consumer research. And by all means, pay close attention to your competitors' efforts.

For consistent creative execution, begin by mapping out your needs with a creative brief. Then give it to your art director, copywriter, and all involved for buy-in—and then stick with it.

Finally, be bold and provocative, and employ attention-getting, risk-taking opportunities that match your experiential visitor offerings with the customers' needs. Properly executed, this approach is bound to separate you from much of today's mundane marketing communications work.

It's an exciting opportunity. You'll cut through the communications clutter out there and really help convey a more enriching and memorable brand that'll pay ongoing dividends for your destination.

The Creative Brief

Project name _____ Date _____
Originating department_____
Project originator _____
Project description (size, shape, look, & feel)_____
Primary service/message _____
Secondary message_____
Competing activity _____
Marketing objective _____
Where is the business coming from? _____
Target audience profile _____
What is the single most important point we can deliver to this audience?

_____
Mandatory inclusions/restrictions _____
Merchandise or distribution plan _____
Timelines_____ # units produced _____
Budget/budget code _____
Approvals (signatures required below from affected depts.) _____

_____
Methods for evaluating success _____

Building Brand Awareness

Today's great brands are best built with public relations, according to the best-selling book, The Fall of Advertising and the Rise of PR, *by Al and Laura Ries. Why? It is because of public relations' higher acceptability from the public as the most believable of all communications media.*

The messages that appear on editorial pages in stories—and not through purchased advertising—consistently garner higher marks with consumers for credibility. For these reasons, newspaper editorial travel sections, consumer travel magazines, and other traditional travel media have a powerful influence over the way Americans plan and choose their vacation travel. And this influence continues to grow, according to recent research studies.

So while you should certainly support your brand with advertising, you should start focusing on PR as the principal marketing vehicle to build your brand. In response to this approach, the current development and expansion of PR publicity programs for DMOs is playing a larger and much more effective role.

Maximizing Destination Publicity

Although many DMOs rely on press releases as the foundation of their media relations programs, the standard PR release format was never designed to effectively produce major feature coverage that can effectively change visitor attitudes and stimulate maximum destination travel interest.

That important requirement is best delivered by on-site writer familiarization for your destination—which is just as essential for your organization as it is for the food writer who actually dines in the restaurant, the sports writer who watches the game, and the cultural writer who views the performance—allowing travel writers to share their personal experiences with readers that best motivate them to make future travel decisions.

Hosting Travel Writers

Conventional wisdom has concluded that the most effective method for writer familiarization is through implementation of individual site inspections or with small parties of no more than a half-dozen writers that give each journalist their own special focus and concentration on their intended interests without having to share story ideas with others.

However, that strategy is extremely time consuming and expensive to replicate if your intention is to produce high volumes of media coverage, particularly from in-depth travel articles.

The most effective method for DMO familiarization is a process first implemented more than twenty years ago by Geiger and Associates (www.geigerpr.com), which plans and hosts larger assemblages of journalists for each of their programs—sometimes in excess of twenty-five or thirty writers per tour.

How do they do it? The key to their success is individually tailored itineraries designed to meet the individual needs of each writer. This requires a disciplined and effective planning process including detailed and segregated tour experiences that intrigue each writer and fulfill special needs. Accomplishing this labor-intensive process also requires increased special assistance and hand-holding for each writer from the PR firm's staff, but the results for this process can consistently be positive and extremely productive.

Familiarization Process Benefits

For the DMO, this approach provides the optimal, cost-efficient way to develop media tours by ultimately reaching millions of potential visitors in your targeted national and regional markets. However, it is a program that requires the skill sets of the seasoned PR firm in support of staff efforts. And not many of them follow this best practice.

Group media tours averaging twenty-two journalists per trip will provide about fifty DMO business partners the opportunity to be featured in major editorial coverage about the destination and drive business to their lodging properties, restaurants, attractions, or other activities.

Media tours with four to eight optional activity tracks occurring simultaneously allow many tourism industry members (beyond a destination's most recognizable and iconic products) to participate. This also allows each journalist to customize the visitation experience and provides for a more intimate and noncompetitive editorial research experience. If the media tour is hosted properly, the DMO pays nothing for the expenses of the media visit and reaps substantial amounts of influential and favorable media coverage in key markets.

A skillfully developed media tour should provide sponsored air transportation, lodging, meals, and activities. (Geiger, for example, tells their destination clients that if they can't obtain sponsored air transportation for the journalists they invite, then they will pay for it themselves.)

Unfortunately, many DMOs don't understand that it is possible to coordinate media tours with all on-site set up and all sponsorship arrangements made by the PR firm. An important prerequisite is that the PR firm must first get to know the destination and its tourism industry partners well enough to develop intricate media tour itineraries, set up the tours, and pitch the destination effectively to the targeted journalists.

The most successful DMOs that undertake programs of this type coordinate several media tours in the course of a year during different seasons. This gives the destination an opportunity to highlight various types of seasonal offerings and involve a larger number of tourism industry partners. The resulting editorial coverage is more broad-based and then continually appears over the course of a year. For more information, contact Debbie Geiger at debbie.geiger@geigerpr.com.

Waldo County: An Unlikely Tourism Success Case Study

Imagine quaint historic villages in coastal Maine. Victorian ships captains' houses as B&Bs. Pristine historic districts, lighthouses, flower farms and orchards, antique shops, scenic drives, and waterfront restaurants serving traditional Maine seafood. Sounds idyllic, but until recently, this remarkable place had never been marketed for tourism.

These twenty-four small communities shared a past as part of a thriving shipbuilding center in the 1800s. However, with the advent of iron-hulled ships, this wood-based shipbuilding region slid into decline. Later, spurred by a strong supply of cheap labor, the poultry-processing industry took hold. New chicken factories began pumping slaughterhouse waste directly into the Atlantic. Most sea life died, and the odor of factories carried for miles as chicken feathers blew down streets like a snow storm. Property values plummeted. Residents thought things couldn't get much worse, and then a torrent of media coverage labeled Waldo County as "the most polluted place in New England." By the mid-1980s, the poultry processing plants shut down, and seemingly overnight, Waldo County's economy died.

Yet today it has undergone a true rebirth, with tourism now thriving as a vital and growing industry. The media branding campaign, featuring on-site travel writer familiarization, was produced by Geiger and Associates and designed to create visibility for this "new" destination. It capitalized on Waldo County's affordability, educating potential visitors about the scope of tourist offerings to increase length of stay, and offsetting years of negative publicity. Nearly 1,000 newspaper and magazine articles have been published in targeted geographic and demographic markets throughout the United States and Canada, with publicity reaching more than 308 million readers with equivalent ad lineage value estimated at $8.8 million.

Results in a seven-year period:

- Overnight occupancy increased 72 percent.

- Length of stay was up 42 percent.
- Restaurant sales increased 65 percent.
- Retail sales increased 58 percent.
- State restaurant and lodging tax collections in Waldo County increased 58 percent—the largest tax increase of any county in Maine for each of the seven years that this innovative program has been in place.

Note: There is no DMO operating in the community, and this media familiarization publicity program is the only marketing initiative employed there—strong testimony to its effectiveness.

The Internet

The Internet has surpassed all communications processes and programs in its ability to provide travel information and influence vacation travel decisions. It is also the most critically important component for the future of destination marketing.

For the first time in history, the Internet allows all of us to be significantly more successful by providing large amounts of useful and motivational information to massive numbers of potential visitors. Another major feature for smaller destinations is that the Internet has more than leveled the competitive playing field, allowing them to become relatively visible and important.

Some of the most important things the Internet can do include

- produce more customer awareness, destination interest, and desire to visit
- efficiently produce more visitors at lower costs
- measure and evaluate your performance success and ROI
- create consumer advocacy for your destination.

Here are fundamental issues required to assure Internet-marketing success.

Issue 1. Developing a Professional Internet Audit

Securing optimal Internet performance should begin with a professional audit and assessment. Such a program from a top tourism industry technology expert would review comparative destination websites and their results, thoroughly evaluate the effectiveness of your current site, and provide a plan of clear directional guidance for the future.

Three expert firms for development of this internal audit, and the Internet marketing plan that follows, are www.ebrains.travel, www.usdm.net, and www.travelspike.com. These two programs may be bundled and offered in the $7,500–$12,500 range.

Issue 2. Producing an Internet Marketing Plan

Rather than just assigning the role of a staff webmaster to oversee your website needs, you will best assure long-term competitive success by hiring an expert to develop a strategic Internet marketing plan. This critically important initiative should be produced to enhance success through further optimizing your destination's web presence, building awareness, boosting traffic, maximizing customer relationship programs, encouraging online transactions, and delivering performance tracking and reporting.

Such a plan is best outsourced by DMOs to either a qualified Internet marketing company or advertising agency. Its principal deliverables would include

- target audiences by various segments, interests, and preferences
- online brand assessment of market share of activity relative to competition
- potential reach through communication channels
- goals, objectives, and metrics for performance planning and delivery
- annual search engine marketing plan
- annual display advertising plan
- annual online PR plan
- annual social marketing plan
- annual mobile marketing plan
- potential online media schedule to create new awareness for the website
- text marketing campaigns
- new packaging strategies.

Also high on the list is a comprehensive registered user program developed today for a number of destination websites. The program objective is to cultivate, over time, new consumer interest in visiting the destination through e-mail newsletters and other techniques sent from the website. It should be feasible for the registered user program to produce email subscribers and repeat visitors to the website over time that could later reasonably produce new destination visitation at the conversion rate of at least 50 percent.

If destination brands are indeed best built with PR / earned impressions and sustained with advertising, then the third supportive initiative should be the integration of Internet ad outreach as a supplement. Its primary advantage, compared to traditional media, is its commanding capability to produce visitors at lower costs.

Keep in mind that the bottom-line importance of conversion of visitors from advertising programs is not in the total number of inquiries received, or even the rate of conversion. Instead, it is the actual cost you must pay for converting each visitor. High dollar costs per converted visitor means that a DMO's limited budget will yield fewer visitors. In contrast, lower conversion costs can produce more successful opportunities for achieving higher volumes of visitors and resulting revenue.

For this reason, DMOs should conclude there is a fundamental strategic interest in employing efficient advertising that is capable of providing lower cost per visitor produced.

That opportunity is principally found in online advertising, which converts visitors (at rates of 50 to 60 percent) at current online costs of between $2.50 to $5.00 per inquiry compared to

- television pay-per-inquiry converted visitors (45 to 60 percent conversion rate) at costs of $12 to $15 each
- magazine "bingo card" leads (45 to 60 percent conversion rate) at costs of $8 to $15 each
- traditional newspaper and magazine advertising costs (30 to 60 percent conversion rate) usually in excess of $25 to $30 to produce a new visitor.

Internet advertising also has a strong advantage over traditional magazine, newspaper, TV, and radio advertising because of its ability to rapidly and accurately track and convert actual destination visitors. It can also be much more efficient. The Internet is also where over 80 percent of travel is researched and planned.

We mentioned that online ad programs can reliably produce consumer inquiries at costs in the $2.50 to $5.00 range. So even with a two to three times higher traditional ad conversion rate compared to that of online advertising, that still means greater volumes of guaranteed visitors can be consistently produced via the Internet for far less than through a traditional print campaign.

In our findings, the optimum program for mining visitors via the Internet is produced by eBrains, Inc., which provides state-of-the-art programs for numerous DMOs, including CVBs and state travel programs. (For more information, see the relevant case history in chapter 5 on "Developing Market Share.")

Issue 3. Measuring Website Performance Success and ROI

Now that you've conducted your website assessment, developed your resulting Internet marketing plan, and launched your enhanced site, it's time to determine its performance results: producing incremental visitors to your destination from its efforts with a strong ROI.

The analysis should also quantify and benchmark the effectiveness of your website, including a demographic and psychographic profile of website users, as well as an analysis of their travel intentions and behaviors. This will help you improve consumer decision making regarding content development and guide future advertising efforts.

Our review of a number of firms, methodologies, and client results concludes that one of the industry's most accurate and defensible models is offered by Destination Analysts, Inc. They follow a comprehensive methodology involving a two-step survey process. Here's how it works:

- **First, a survey invitation is placed on your website's main entry pages** and presented to a random sampling of web traffic. A brief questionnaire obtains key information: planned trip type, the consumer's point-in-time in the travel decision-making process, the expected date of arrival, and an opt-in request to survey them later.

- **The follow-up survey is sent by e-mail to the intercept survey opt-ins** at the end of their expected stays in your community, and the questionnaire collects all additional data needed for ROI analysis—including specific visitor characteristics, behavior, travel activity, and spending.
- **Analysis and reports then follow, focusing on economic impact** derived specifically from visitors who had not fully made up their minds to visit when they initially came to the website, and including only those trips or extended stays, based on the website's effectiveness. Your report includes comprehensive study findings highlighted by visitor trips, expenditures, and resulting ROI.

It takes a minimum six-month survey period to collect adequate sampling, and a full year is considered ideal to capture any seasonality in destination travel patterns. As for potential results, Destination Analysts anticipates that for every 1,000 unique visitors to the website, estimated annual economic effect generated for the destination would be about $16,000.

For those wishing to economize analysis costs, apply economic data estimates for at least two successive years before deploying a new study. For comprehensive information, including project timelines and in-depth methodologies, e-mail ROI@destinationanalysts.com or call 415-307-3283 or 415-716-7983.

Social Media

With Facebook's more than 750 million active users and Twitter's 200 million users generating 350 million tweets and 1.6 billion search queries daily—not to mention 150 million blogs—DMOs are assessing where they should be in developing a social media presence that can extend their brands.

Social media is about connections between people. Travel and tourism is also about connections between people. Therefore, social media and tourism are rapidly becoming old pals. Yet, if you ask a dozen destination marketers the definition of social media, you'll most likely get a dozen different responses.

Still, social media has dramatically transformed the way people communicate, search for information, make decisions, socialize, learn, and share experiences. This also applies to consumer behavior in travel and tourism.

While in the past, DMOs were the principal creators and owners of the content, today the consumer is creating much of the content. There are ever-growing numbers of travelers who search and consume travel information created by other travelers for their travel planning, and then share their experiences when they return from their trips. Given the emerging experiential nature of tourism, the information created by other travelers is even more important and influential in the search and decision-making process than when considering other types of purchases.

Establishing the Value of Social Media

The challenge is determining to what extent specific benefits are accrued to destinations—and particularly, the performance productivity that is generated from social media.

Social media is certainly all the rage, with more people getting serious about marketing, with more dollars now being devoted to social media. A lot of DMOs are running to social media as fast as they can because they are afraid that if they don't, they'll get left far behind.

Integrating social media into your marketing plan may have long-term benefits—keeping your destination in front of the consumer while building a key relationship with them for long-term success. But be aware that there is a productive way to approach social media, and alternatively, there is an approach to avoid.

Before you take the plunge, do some basic in-house research to confirm where your destination is in relationship to your competitors in the arena of social media. What are they doing that you aren't? How is it working for them and their stakeholders? And, do they really even know?

Following the crowd is not the way to go. DMOs who have built impressive social media platforms have done so with a social media strategy for consumer engagement, not merely fans. It takes budget, but it also takes a proven strategy.

I often hear this statement from social media proponents, "We know there's an ROI," they begin, "but tracking this social media networking expenditure is difficult." What many are really saying is: accurate performance productivity is illusive; they can't currently provide reliable evaluative research that assesses ROI or performance delivered as measured in new visitors and related spending.

Searching for Answers

I've asked numerous travel research experts if they were aware of any major studies that quantifiably measure social media's influence and end results in the travel decision-making process. The answer to date has always been no. However, tracking the behavior of your social media fans may be an effective way to gauge value. As examples:

- Are requests for visitor guides being tracked as an indication of a future visit? If so, social media fans who request visitor guides can be measured for future visitation value.
- Are click-throughs to members or destination partners or advertisers measured? If so, social media fans who click-through can potentially be measured and valued in the same way.

Make the Distinction Between Social Networking and Electronic PR

One component of social media that can indeed be tracked for ROI is the development of electronic PR / media publicity. You should think of that as a separate and distinct marketing initiative of social media—tracking and evaluating it the same way you evaluate traditional PR and media publicity: through media impressions produced and their estimated value against paid advertising, with return of visitor impressions based on your investment in marketing dollars expended.

However, while we can confirm from numerous research studies that traditional PR/publicity receives the highest ratings for consumer believability and in motivating travel decision making, no similar research is available that clarifies those attributes on a projectable basis for social PR/media publicity.

We also hear from social media marketers that higher levels of social media are now being used for travel planning. Obviously, tourism marketers can't afford to ignore social media; they just have to carefully think about how to take advantage of it in order to exercise influence on travelers.

Here are some interesting observations about the popularity and the trust factors of social media by Dr. Ulrike Gretzel, associate professor of marketing, the Institute for Innovation in Business and Social Research, University of Wollongong,

Wollongong, Australia. Dr. Gretzel is well recognized for her research regarding social media. Her comments follow:

- *What is popular? What has the most influence?* Online travel reviews, such as hotel reviews posted on TripAdvisor, are particularly popular sources of information. Activity choices and restaurant decisions are also increasingly affected by the opinions of review writers, while decisions on where to travel are typically made before reviews are consulted. Other social media types, such as videos and podcasts, are generally less influential, although gender and age differences come into play when looking at the influence of specific social media categories.

- *Do travelers blindly trust the opinions of strangers?* Our research indicates that trust levels are very high, that a considerable number even prefer the opinions of unknown people over the opinions of friends and relatives. However, many consumers are also aware of marketers posting reviews or paying professional review writers.

- *Do tourism marketers have to worry?* Our studies find that a majority of travelers think that social media contents are more up-to-date, more fun to read, more interesting, more relevant, more comprehensive, more specific, and more helpful in making decisions than information provided by tourism marketers. However, Dr. Gretzel concludes, that does *not* mean that marketers no longer provide an important function. The travelers we surveyed actually trust social media content more if it is provided on official destination marketing websites.

That's certainly another strong vote of confidence for DMOs.

Going Forward, Be Diligent

Eventually, you will need to develop a social media strategy. Here's a brief checklist of important tips from Leah Woolford, founder and chairman of USDM.net:

- The DMO social media strategy should be developed to work in concert with other objectives, and it should have a scorecard for measurement, both objective and subjective.
- The social strategy must include the stakeholders. Their participation is key to success.
- A budget should be allocated to social media. Real campaigns are not free, and those are the ones that move the needle and have the greatest ROI potential.

Develop an Entry-Level Review

If and when you decide to pursue a formalized social media plan, your first step should be to hire a reputable firm to develop an entry-level review.

This approach should follow the same process you should always employ in website development—hiring an expert to assure that your Internet marketing plan is properly assessed and then integrated with your comprehensive DMO marketing plan.

In the case of social media, the initial entry-level review should include

- **monitoring and evaluating** where you rank in the social media marketplace against major competitors
- **creating a social media plan cost–benefit analysis** for what they can produce and its anticipated results through a ROI analysis
- **reviewing your existing marketing plan** to determine how and where the recommended new social media initiatives will support your existing consumer market reach, frequency of message, and anticipated visitor expansion.

Expert firms for potential development of this social media entry review are www.ebrains.travel, www.travelspike.com, and www.usdm.net.

Delivering and Managing Performance

"In the absence of clearly defined goals," a business expert once wryly observed, "we become strangely loyal to performing daily acts of trivia." For most DMOs, producing quantifiable performance results, through goal-setting, is at the very core of its mission—and the principal delivery system for evaluating the bottom-line success of your organization.

There's little doubt that today's DMO fulfills a litany of important work for the industry and our communities that other organizations can't replicate:

- It is at the forefront of enhancing visitor support of quality of life issues and resulting amenities for residents as well, some of which would probably not exist without the business generated by visitors.
- Through destination marketing initiatives, such as advertising and sales that produce new visitors, the DMO helps create local jobs and generates local taxes that may materially reduce the requirement for additional resident taxes.
- It also increases the economic impact to the destination from new visitors that would have gone elsewhere except for the marketing efforts of its staff.

However, the principal requirement for successful performance is the quantifiable production of DMO results in response to its marketing efforts.

The *Handbook of Destination Marketing (DMAI) Performance Standards for CVBs*, which we assisted in developing as a member of its performance measurement team, says it best:

> In a perfect world . . . a CVB would know exactly how many of its destination's visitors were motivated to come solely by its efforts. And further, which of its marketing efforts were responsible for that visitor. However, the CVB and its local tourism industry don't exist in a perfect world. Instead, potential visitors are constantly bombarded by such a myriad of stimuli (the CVB, its industry partners, national sales offices, the media, and so on) that it becomes impossible to say that a visitor was motivated 100% by the CVB and only by the CVB.

In practice, when addressing the issue of visitors generated and their positive economic impacts, the CVB should, at the very least, have in place monitoring and research programs that identify visitors and visitor spending that were *clearly and significantly* generated by its efforts. . . . The CVB should also adopt a conservative approach when determining the number of visitors generated by its efforts to ensure that its stated ROI is credible and can stand up to external scrutiny.

Monitoring Performance with a Tracking System Report

An initial step in performance management is development of a comprehensive tracking report to monitor and report the DMO's ongoing successes, measuring both key specific marketing activity and performance that it produces.

This ongoing report can also be supplemented by a brief narrative summary and should be produced monthly, then reported either monthly or quarterly, as well as in a year-end summary that compares its success to former past year's results.

This new performance tracking report becomes the measurement response to the DMO mission statement. It should singularly be the most important tool used for measuring ongoing DMO performance and as a guide in future goal-setting. It should be disseminated to principal constituents, made available as part of government contracts, and used to highlight the organization's next annual report, marketing plan, and other communications programs for the community.

The report's enclosed marketing measures should be provided in two categories:

- marketing activity
- marketing performance productivity.

Marketing activity includes such work as literature distributed, visitors serviced at the information center, sales calls made, leads issued, etc. As more promotional activity is produced and targeted appropriately, there should be corresponding increases, over time in marketing productivity.

Marketing performance productivity is the most important output for DMOs. These business measurements include conventions and sports functions booked and resulting room night revenue, hotel reservations made and resulting economic impact, as well as other important results of the organization's successful marketing efforts on behalf of the community. Whenever feasible, performance productivity measures should be forecast and stated as goals to be delivered, and so should activity, such as sales leads generated, which can then convert to business booked. Next, take these steps:

- Group and list the performance productivity measures.
- Provide estimated economic impacts. Some DMOs produce annual estimates of economic results from these programs based on their in-house

studies that are generated by the same staff that were also compensated for delivering the program results—a process that is at best suspect.

- Whenever feasible, contract with third-party independent research firms to assure validation of estimated results. This can include market research companies, universities with a proven track record of producing research studies, accounting firms, or consultants who specialize in projects requiring a research component.
- Include detailed footnotes for each estimate of performance return, with explanations that help readers understand the methodologies employed to produce the results.
- Provide productivity measurements in the form of future annual goals to be achieved, following the development of benchmarked first-year results.

Performance Productivity Categories for a Tracking System Report

Here are the categories for your use, dependent on markets to be reached:

New Conventions and Meetings Booked
Estimated room nights generated
Resulting economic impact

Convention Center Bookings (from customers using that facility)
Estimated room nights generated
Resulting economic impact

Sports Event Development
Number of events, participants, and room nights

Estimates/Methodology: A newly developed Event Impact Calculator from DMAI measures the economic value of an event and calculates its ROI to local taxes. The program for DMOs has been developed by Tourism Economics, an Oxford Economics Company. The models are based on city-specific data, based on various types of events and other criteria, and updated annually.

New Group Leisure Tour Programs Booked
Number of programs
Estimated participants
Attendant room nights

Estimates/Methodology: economic impact reported with input from tour operators who produced the programs

Leisure Visitors Produced through Website-Based Programs

Estimated economic impact
Visitor and visitor parties produced
Room nights generated

Estimates/Methodology: produced by website and validated by third party

Leisure Visitors Produced through Advertising Programs

Visitor/visitor parties produced
Room nights generated
Estimated economic impact

Estimates/Methodology: provided by independent third-party conversion study validation

Positive Traditional Media Publicity Impressions

Readership (circulation)/viewers/listeners
Resulting $ value as estimated in costs for advertising lineage

Estimates/Methodology: provided through third-party estimates

Positive Electronic Social Media Publicity Impressions

Readership
Resulting $ value

Other Social Media Programs

Based on new methodologies to be determined, potentially being developed by DMAI as new industry performance standards

Film Office

production shoots assisted
Economic impact produced from film production

Estimates/Methodology: requires third-party validation

Membership/Partnership Development

Total number of partners
New members
Retention rate
Annual $ support

Estimates/Methodology: by staff, validated by finance and admin.

Partnership In-Kind Services Achieved in $ Equivalency

Estimated total $ amount

Number of support programs (hosted travel writers, airfare, client accommodations, advertising, partner function support, etc.)

Estimates/Methodology: by staff, validated by finance and admin.

Convention Services Quality and Effectiveness

Quality standards, to be based on follow-up customer satisfaction survey including qualitative criteria for the meeting planner

Estimates/Methodology: produced by staff, third-party evaluation

Visitor Welcome Center

Room nights produced
Economic impact generated

Estimates/Methodology: through third-party analysis

Adding DMO Marketing Activity

Next, include in this tracking system report your ongoing monthly and annual results for DMO activity that are also vital to the program, including many of the following if these are programs produced by your DMO.

Sales Calls Made

Meeting planners
Tour operators
Convention planners
Sports decision makers
Travel writers

Trade Shows Attended

Meetings and conventions
Tour operators
Sports development

General Marketing

Advertising impressions produced
Consumer inquiries generated and serviced
Collateral publications distributed
Media publicity press releases issued
Media inquiries serviced

Website
Unique visitors/user sessions
Page views
Registered users

Visitor Services
Visitors serviced at information centers
Inquiries processed (by category, including advertising, the web, etc.)

Convention Center Facility Leads Generated
Estimated room nights
Potential economic value

Convention Hotel Leads Generated
Estimated room nights
Potential economic value
Convention bid proposals produced
Percentage conversion of sales leads to business booked

Sports Leads
Estimated room nights
Potential economic impact

Tour Operator Group Sales Leads
Estimated room nights
Potential economic value

Total Sales Leads Generated
Total estimated room nights
Potential economic value

Sales Calls / Client Contacts Made
Meeting planners
Tour operators
Travel writers/media
Sports development

Familiarization Tours Conducted
Meeting planners
Clients participating
Tour operators
Clients participating

Travel writers
Clients participating (include potential value where available)

Site Inspections Hosted (individual trips—track value if booked)
Meeting planners
Tour operators
Travel writers
(include potential value where available)

Convention Services
Conventions serviced
Housing nights serviced
Revenue generated

Additional Annual Inputs
Lost and canceled business reports

Developing the Optimum Goal-Setting Process

Several years ago, while helping to develop a performance-based plan for a CVB that was known for its take-order, reactive culture, the vice president of PR appeared perplexed about the new planning process.

"Would you please explain for me why it's necessary for us to count all the writers we hosted last year?" he asked.

"Well, how many *did you host*?" I responded.

"A lot! Well, actually, I don't know the exact number."

"And how many do you anticipate hosting for the year ahead?" I asked, while parenthetically adding, "And by the way, don't you think it might be a good idea for us to set that number as a performance goal to be achieved by your department for the new year ahead?"

He began to get the picture.

The setting of performance goals guides all of us to achieve higher performance for the future. The process initially begins following the benchmarking of first-year results—and wherever your initiatives can influence and forecast future achievements. Now you should begin preparation to produce performance-based goals to be sought for the new year ahead.

Setting SMART Goals

Share with staff and stakeholders this description of **S-M-A-R-T** goals: **S**pecific, **M**easurable, **A**ttainable, **R**ealistic, and **T**imely.

Goals, of course, are only required when they can be effectively managed to achieve results produced by the staff. So, for example, goals would not be established for achieving specific numbers of visitors at the visitor welcome center or for specific total numbers of website visitors; in these cases, and others, the staff has no ability to affect positive goal outcomes and performance.

Begin with Benchmarking

For the most effective goal forecasting and delivery system, individual staff should be encouraged to initially develop measurable goals from the bottom up, using the benchmarking report and other market data, competitive information, and market funding parameters as guides. This approach provides staff members the opportunity to envision their own targets and commit to delivery. Then a collaborative effort should be conducted with management for any goal adjustments in relationship to current market support and market conditions.

I once worked with a major DMO whose board of directors had taken it upon themselves to set quantifiable goals for the staff. They did that for five long years, and not once was the staff able to attain them. Why? Because the goals were unrealistic and unachievable, not based on market conditions and, therefore, received no buy-in from the staff. You can imagine how staff morale was adversely affected by this inappropriate process—and how pleased they became when they were finally allowed to chart their own course. As a result, performance has increased each year since.

Keep in mind that your goals should never be set in stone. Weak market conditions during the year may require an ongoing periodic, realistic reassessment and the lowering of annual goals. And correspondingly, reaching an intended annual goal early in the year—say by the third quarter—should call for a readjustment.

Providing Qualitative Staff Goals

In addition to the quantitative performance deliverables, staff qualitative goals can be incorporated annually as part of each employee's job description and then listed in the marketing plan.

They can be included as requisites for staff completion for the year ahead and should be referred to as "personal performance objectives." This is because unlike traditional quantifiable goals, these come under the category of qualitative task-oriented work. Examples may include program development, increasing contact lists, and completion of special training programs.

Creating a Dynamite Marketing Plan

An effective marketing plan can do a lot more than provide a road map for success. It can forge strong community alliances, foster team spirit, and strengthen common purpose throughout your operation and community.

My definition of a dynamite marketing plan is one built from the ground up—with a zero-base budget and absolutely no rules—except to reach for performance success across all departments, with full team support and a belief that the final plan belongs to everyone on the staff.

In the spirit of collaboration, you should involve key community leaders and constituent groups. Their input will be helpful in producing an inclusionary process while validating your initiatives on their behalf.

Be sure that each department head actually supervises their department's plan input. I've known some supervisors who actually tried to turn over the whole project to subordinates, sending a strong signal that this project wasn't theirs to support. And that will quickly abdicate leadership and tear down morale.

The Marketing Plan Model Outline

The following marketing plan model should be used as a guide for staff direction:

- **Begin with an executive summary that does not exceed a couple of pages**. Prepared by the CEO or chief marketing officer, the executive summary should succinctly point out that the plan resulted from collaborative dialogue and input from key community hospitality constituents. Their names should also be noted.

- **Explain the destination consolidated marketing process**. New visitor business can best be attracted to your community through coordinated group action rather than through individual actions. Thus, your office acts as a cooperative, representing all components of the community's visitor industry (hotels, restaurants, convention facilities, tour operators, attractions, transportation carriers, retail, and others who are vitally important to visitors). This destination sales team approach makes your organization more effective in carrying out a comprehensive, unified marketing program to benefit the community.

- **Include bullet point goal highlights** proposed in the plan, if your timetable allows their announcement. If not, include other major highlights on a departmental basis. The executive summary you've just created has now become the blueprint for your media release of the marketing plan to the community.

- **Awards and recognitions follow**. Take a page to list recent accolades bestowed by the industry on your operation or on individual staffers. And if you don't have recognitions to share, make it a point to begin earning them.

- **Now you're ready for the introduction**. Include your marketing mission, your visioning statement, and your strategic process to deliver a research-based, customer-focused, market-driven, and brand-oriented program that produces quantifiable performance success.

- **List the organization's major objectives** regarding generating awareness, stimulating customer interest and desire, advocating for travel development, supporting member businesses, etc.

- **Follow these objectives with a section on destination branding** and everyone's role in its important culturization process.

The principal building blocks of your plan follow, including sections on

- **marketplace complications:** all the impediments or roadblocks to success, including perceived complications
- **marketplace opportunities:** show where the new doors to success can be opened
- **major challenges:** competitive city hotel inventories, larger marketing budgets that limit your program's ability to create customer share of mind and market, additional negative influences
- **department inputs:** each department, office, or program effort should be addressed and include

  - a brief departmental mission
  - a section on national trends affecting work
  - planned highlights for the year ahead
  - the new year's annual sales goals in firm numbers, comparing them to the work of the current year
  - each market segment and each department's marketplace complications and competitive analysis
  - the primary target audiences to be reached for each major strategy and the tactics or work programs to accomplish each strategy

- **a comprehensive marketing calendar:** listing all major strategies by month, containing

  - trade shows, sales forums, and sales missions (when and by whom)
  - media relations publicity to be produced
  - advertising and direct mail to be placed
  - publications / collateral to be produced
  - major membership/partnership development initiatives.

- **a line item budget:** major expenditures by function, including income funding sources

Now return to the front cover. With the help of some creative staff input, develop a visionary title for your new marketing plan that captures the essence of what you have just created—new beginnings and new opportunities for performance success. With what you've now accomplished in this plan, some great titles should spring to mind.

Do you have a contract with government? If you operate with a formalized written government agreement, this marketing plan, along with its annual goals to be achieved, should be provided as an annual addendum to the contract.

CHAPTER 2
Strategic Planning

"If you don't know where you are going, you'll end up someplace else."

–Yogi Berra

Long-Range Planning

Hockey Hall of Famer Wayne Gretsky described his objective this way: "I skate to where the puck is going to be—not to where it's been." Keeping your eye on the future—and preparing for it through long-range planning—is the very essence of DMO strategic planning.

Strategic plans are long-range, big-picture plans that are designed with the fundamental goal of providing a longer term strategy for achieving DMO and community success. These strategic plans come in many shapes and sizes and can deliver diverse outcomes.

In considering the development of your strategic plan, you should discuss the general needs you wish to see fulfilled and gauge their components with your executive committee or board. Perhaps you have copies of other plans that have some of the characteristics you'd like to emulate.

Questions, Answers, Other Considerations

Here is a brief review of issues that can bring you closer to determining the kind of plan you need and the implementation process to follow:

- **Accomplishments:** Have you or others identified what should be accomplished with this plan—any broad-based issues or challenges for future consideration and special potential outcomes that this plan should address or achieve? That isn't a requisite for plan development, but reviewing challenges, impediments, and opportunities may better frame answers to other questions.

- **Problems and issues:** Your plan should solve them, not just list them. So instead of just reviewing challenges and opportunities, your plan should provide detailed solutions and strategic directional steps to overcome these impediments and help chart your positive future direction. Simply stated, a strategic plan without answers is not really a strategic plan.

- **Participants:** What is the scope of this plan? Is its focus narrowly defined for the DMO so that it can be accomplished with the primary guidance of your board, its committees, the staff, and stakeholders/membership? Or does your plan anticipate dealing with major community issues that transcend the DMO and also require input, guidance, and support from other constituent groups? Who might they include? Government administration and other agencies or departments, business leadership, the chamber of commerce, the arts council, colleges, and universities? Who else? Collaboration is important here; dependent on needs, don't leave anyone out.

- **Duration of plan:** What is your required time schedule to complete the plan, and what are the anticipated costs for plan completion? Detailed plans can be completed within a six- to nine-month time frame; others should require much less time. As for costs, some planning documents with limited, focused agendas can be completed for several thousand dollars and can scale upward to complex programs and deliverables costing several hundreds of thousands of dollars.

- **Management or organizational support:** Will you deliver the process in-house with existing staff or develop an RFP to hire a strategic planning firm for turn-key strategic support, meeting development, research and analysis, and final report preparation?

- **Strategic planning committee:** You may include members of your executive committee or the board, along with key staff and stakeholders, but the strategic planning committee should have its own identity and be responsible for the fulfillment of its oversight mission.

- **Support competencies:** If you decide to hire outside support for development of your strategic plan, be sure to hire strategic thinkers. Even if your needs are limited and you only require a facilitator, make sure the individual is a strategic thinker. If you don't, the person won't have the required skills and abilities to add value to your planning process by applying the true depth of strategic understanding to adequately deal with a variety of needs expressed throughout the process.

What Is Strategic Thinking?

Strategic thinking is the way people think about, view, and create the future. It is a lot more than responding to day-to-day and long-term problems. It is proactive, not reactive. And it focuses on creating a better future and adding value.

Two prerequisites for strategic thinking support are to find individuals or firms with

- **a track record of achievement in destination marketing,** or at the very least, marketing execution or market planning in some phase of tourism

- **depth of knowledge** about current industry best business practices, markets, research, and other complementary requisites for destination planning.

Other general attributes of strategic thinkers include

- **being flexible thinkers**, having the ability to move out of their comfort zone and use new, broader thinking for planning, analyzing, and evaluating
- **being passionate** about what they do and having a deep source of energy and motivation
- **having the special ability to define and plan at various levels** before deciding how to best achieve final results
- **not being limited** by current paradigms
- **possessing the ability** to develop a clear vision and then applying that vision as the foundation for strategic thinking and planning.

With these attributes, it's clear to see why strategic thinkers are best equipped to think about change and imagine the results we can positively achieve in the future through strategic planning. That's why you may need them to round out your team.

Make the plan a living document, through an effective, ongoing process that can assure the implementation of its recommendations throughout its intended time frame / duration. Ongoing task force meetings related to their special issues should report out their plans, progress, problems, and modifications. At future planning intervals—say every six months—the full strategic planning committee should meet to assess its work, review progress, and modify its plan if needed. After all, strategic planning is never-ending and should always be considered a work in progress.

Here is a brief inventory of components that may be considered for your plan:

- DMO mission statement review
- cascading objections from the mission that clarify the scope of work of the DMO
- vision statement for the DMO of the future
- SWOT (strengths, weaknesses, opportunities, and threats) analysis—I recommend that you replace *threats* with the less ominous sounding *challenges* for producing a SWOC analysis. Also, reorder the analysis components: strengths, weaknesses, challenges, and opportunities. This concludes the exercise on a positive note. A minimum of two SWOC analyses should be conducted, the first exercise solely with the DMO staff, who are usually more knowledgeable, have a good long-term perspective, and will be familiar with available research for

framing issues. Then the second SWOC analysis should be provided for your principal stakeholders

- follow-up meetings for additional input with key stakeholders and community constituents
- customer assessments and input
- stakeholder assessment and input
- national or regional trends and their impacts
- annual tourism economic impact results for the destination with comparisons to other primary competitor DMOs
- competitive set assessments with other DMOs and communities, including DMO marketing budgets, manpower availability, principal product and service attributes, and other advantages, both real and perceived
- other assessment instruments, including lost convention business reports.

Following analysis of fundamental community and DMO need, a centerpiece of many strategic plans is the listing of major challenges, impediments, and opportunities, usually numbering less than ten, that are supported by action plans for remediation. Your issues may include

- competitive funding opportunities
- program and performance enhancement
- relationship community building with government and other constituents
- community revitalization through product development, including master planning and convention center/conference/headquarters hotel needs
- creation of new capacity
- collaboration and leveraging issues
- technology applications for the future
- crisis management issues.

Destination Models

I've included several planning models for review and consideration. You should consider them all, because there's no specific model that stands above all others—and your new strategic planning model, and all it contains, should be strictly about your destination, your special needs, and your desired outcomes.

Below are some highlights of the strategic plans.

The Atlantic City Convention and Visitors Authority Strategic Plan

- Concentrated on defining the agency's role of multiple market positions in the tourism industry

- Delivered a broad community consensus approach that defined community and agency strengths, weaknesses, challenges, and opportunities
- Delivered priority objectives: an eight-point strategic new focus to address challenges and prepare for long-term success

Planning objectives included: Reintroducing the destination for the marketplace, new sales/marketing initiatives for business enhancement, product diversification requirements, development of new marketing resources, producing new customer awareness, enhancing customer service, expanding partnership alliances, and developing a long-range visioning process.

The Los Angeles Convention and Visitors Bureau Strategic Marketing Plan

- Developed as a community-wide consensus plan to develop support for new funding that would grow visitor volume during the three-year period for conventions and meetings, along with domestic and international leisure markets
- Incorporated requirements for new research, provided a broad-based industry assessment, and listed objectives, strategies, and specific action plans to produce desired results

The Greater Miami Convention and Visitors Bureau Strategic Plan

- Incorporated extensive recent performance audit summaries of the agency
- Provided detailed sales and marketing strategies to produce desired outcomes
- Highlighted agency accountability in its performance measures and ROI for the community
- Aligned budgets and implementation tactics
- Reviewed current annual performance goals for sales, service, governance, funding, infrastructure, community relations, and service/attitude

The Pennsylvania Tourism Office Strategic Tourism Master Plan

- Coalesced broad-based stakeholder interests through a series of input sessions across the state
- Incorporated a master plan for future success that included institutional enhancement, promotion, human resources, infrastructure, policy environment, and product development
- Offered a detailed analysis of industry "Best tourism industry practices" from California, Florida, Illinois, Virginia, Kentucky, and Arkansas

Just remember that you have a lot of options. And your own—and perhaps unique—strategic plan approach can be built by drawing on any or all of these models.

When You're Finished, It's Time to Begin Again

This strategic planning process is never really over. Reflection and updates should be continuous and planned at agreed-upon intervals. If there is a final piece of advice to give, it would be: focus more on learning and less on the methods.

When you have finally completed the first strategic plan's time frame, it'll be time for developing your next strategic plan. But this time around—thanks to your new-found expertise—you and the DMO will have an even better handle on how to get there with greater efficiencies.

New York TOURISM 2000:
A Strategic Plan Case Study of Economic Recovery

In the fall of 1990, "The rotting of the Big Apple" was *Time* magazine's penetrating cover story that chronicled the city's rising fear about crime, crumbling infrastructure, and social decay. Nowhere was it felt more than throughout the city's tourism industry, which was reeling from exorbitant tourism taxes that had risen to 21 ¼ percent, diminishing convention and leisure travel and resulting in lower hotel occupancy. Many local tourism leaders viewed this period as a classic case of "killing the goose that laid the golden egg."

In response to these issues, the New York Convention and Visitors Bureau launched its first strategic plan. Its mission: to devise strategies for enhancing the city's tourism infrastructure to accommodate the next generation of visitors. A committee of twenty-one prominent New York tourism and community leaders was established to provide guidelines and input. Six workshops were held, and more than four hundred leaders of business, government, and citizen groups were invited to participate from the five boroughs. Follow-up mailings to hundreds of additional individuals and associations solicited ideas. In response, the plan featured six strategic goals supported by more than four dozen detailed strategies for addressing them.

At the conclusion of the process, and following public release of the plan, NYC Convention and Visitors Bureau Chairman Arthur Surin urged leaders to step up to the challenge. "It's now time for government and industry to review this strategic plan, embrace its strategies, and be part of the implementation process." They did just that, and major achievements that followed included

- reducing the hotel transient occupancy tax by 5 percent, which had become a major deterrent to visitation
- creating city marketing support for the CVB for the first time through a modest dedicated portion of the hotel occupancy tax and not annually through appropriation that had occasionally been reduced based on whim
- focusing and revising the Javits Convention Center's policies, which later produced higher volumes of convention business and greater positive economic returns for the city
- understanding the need for nurturing tourism as one of the city's greatest attributes and revenue streams that led to development of the comprehensive system of business improvement districts.

During the ensuing years, tourism in New York City solidified and expanded its role as a major global tourism destination. Today, as a result, it serves as a major engine of economic development and a strong catalyst for enhancing the quality of life for its residents.

The Successful Board Retreat

With proper advance planning and input from board and staff, you can accomplish some amazing things during your next retreat that'll assure a new foundation for long-range strategic planning.

Mature organizations that regularly schedule retreats are very much aware that a board retreat is a great program for celebration and reflection, an important time to pause and take stock of where everyone wants to go and how to best get there.

It's also a time to build camaraderie and team spirit. Most importantly, the retreat should be an integral step in the process of continuous performance enhancement.

The Retreat Planning Process

Let's review the retreat planning process checklist:

- **Who plans it?** This initial planning exercise should include participants from senior staff and board leadership to plan the retreat.
- **What's the best time frame?** A pragmatic consideration is how much time is available for volunteer participants.
- **What are the meaningful accomplishments?** You should plan to cover a few central issues in some depth that can later be implemented, rather than developing an expanded agenda that may end up being just another general discussion. Can you establish realistic goals and timelines for accomplishment? That should be a prime consideration.
- **Which other stakeholders should be invited?** Depending on your agenda, you may wish to include other community constituents if they have a stake in the issues to be addressed.
- **Who should facilitate?** Retreat success requires the use of a skilled facilitator (and preferably a strategic thinker), one versed in both destination marketing and management. In this way, the organization has an independent industry expert to clarify best business practices, probe and validate directional recommendations, and share competitive perspectives.

Defining the Retreat's Purpose

Next, you'll want to define the actual purpose of the retreat. Some experts suggest that you should focus on the top one to three strategic issues facing the organization. This could include serious deficiencies that you want to tackle, such as competitive funding for destination marketing, relationship management issues with various constituents, new partnership development, or destination branding initiatives.

Many prefer to use the retreat primarily for long-range planning—long-range issues that cannot necessarily be accomplished in one year.

You may also have some management challenges or impediments that adversely affect your organization's performance. They may include oversight micromanagement, a proliferation of subcommittees and task forces that dilute the staff's role, or misunderstandings about the board's job description.

With those considerations in mind, here are recommendations for a traditional one-day board retreat. Working with your staff and board, you can also fine-tune this format to meet your own special needs.

The One-Day Board Retreat

The following one-day approach focuses on four fundamental objectives:

- **introduces participants to the destination marketing industry** and outlines where your organization fits
- **revisits and gains consensus on the organization's mission**, objectives, and vision that lay the foundation for all of your work
- **provides a leadership plan for the organization** and clarifies group and individual roles of the volunteer in relationship to staff
- **gains input from participants** on major unresolved issues and challenges that affect the DMO and its mission.

All this may sound like a lot to cover in one day. But if properly facilitated, this becomes a fast-moving exercise that keeps everyone engaged and consistently gets high marks from participants. However, if some segments aren't required, then you'll have even more time available for the fundamentally important session number four (the SWOC assessment), which is outlined later.

Below is the recommended content for the retreat:

Session 1 (9:00 a.m. – 10:15 a.m.): Today's DMO: An Introduction to the Destination Marketing Industry

Following breakfast, this morning session gets everyone quickly acquainted with the culture of today's DMO and its important role in economic development. Board members are first introduced to the history of the industry and are provided a relevant context for the operation of the organization.

For this introductory session, incorporate highlights of the DMAI Futures Study and review the challenges ahead for DMOs.

Next, follow the outline of the leading CVB industry textbook *Fundamentals of Destination Management and Marketing*.

In this initial session, the board quickly gains an understanding of

- DMO context and industry history
- industry size and scope
- the consolidated approach to destination marketing
- markets and customers
- sales and service
- research
- tactical areas including advertising, technology, web development, direct sales, PR management, and collateral development
- performance delivery and performance management
- stakeholder/member relations.

Session 2 (10:30 a.m. – 12:00 p.m.): Mission, Objectives, and Vision

Following a brief break, the facilitator works with the board to review—and potentially craft—these priority components that provide the genesis for operational management.

Mission. Review the significance of the mission statement. An organization's well-crafted mission should reflect its fundamental purpose and core responsibility. The objective is to review the existing mission statement and get input for an optimum statement. Questions asked should include the following:

- Do you accept responsibility for performance marketing by clearly stating your role in producing new visitor business?
- Are you the official DMO for your community?
- Do you lead a strong public/private partnership for your community?

Objectives. Review the list of broad-based supportive objectives that cascade from the mission, and clarify the parameters of all ongoing work and responsibilities of the organization. This assures that participants won't veer off course in recommending projects that don't fall within the purview of the DMO. All future plans—including strategic plans, the annual marketing plan, business plan, and department and individual performance objectives—can then flow from the mission statement and these broad-based operational objectives.

Vision. To begin this process, the questions posed to the board are as follows: What will the DMO be like in the future, and what values must we embrace to get us there?

This mission, objectives, and vision process will provide the genesis for the new business framework for the organization.

Session 3 (2:00 p.m. – 3:00 p.m.): Board Governance: A Leadership Plan for Success

Following lunch, the board becomes thoroughly acquainted and oriented to its management responsibilities for policy making, administration, and oversight.

Follow the best business practices of the US association management industry as fostered by association executives, as well as best business practices for DMO management.

Time allows for a thorough verbal and written review of how the board should effectively operate—and what standards they should follow in fulfillment of the organization's mission. Areas to be covered include

- **the board job description and governance guidelines**: the traditional tasks of your board in relationship to those of the paid administrator/CEO and staff
- **recommended board governance parameters and style**: how your board should initiate its tasks in a manner that emphasizes outward vision, encourages diverse viewpoints, and provides for strategic and proactive leadership in a clear distinction between board and staff roles
- **code of conduct** and ethics policy for both board and staff.

Section 4 (3:15 p.m. – 5:00 p.m.): The Board SWOC Assessment for Issues Management

After a brief break, the board has an opportunity to roll up its sleeves in this interactive session, framing current issues, concerns, and opportunities as you take the reins for the future success of the organization.

The SWOC exercise provides board input as the members list and discuss the organization's and community's strengths, weaknesses, and challenges; then everyone concentrates on the positive opportunities to ameliorate concerns, capturing and prioritizing strategic issues for your organization, such as funding, regionalization, program content, and the tactics needed for accomplishing them.

This ends the session on an extremely positive and uplifting note.

(After the SWOC analysis, you may determine that some of these issues will require one or more follow-up task forces to further explore key issues and offer solutions with timelines for completion.)

Memorializing the Retreat

Keeping the momentum going for issues covered in your retreat dictates that all actions taken that day should be memorialized in a written planning document.

This written review of the retreat should be the first planning tool you revisit for the future, whether it's during the very next regularly scheduled meeting of the board or when your next annual retreat is being planned twelve months hence.

This written document also gives your constituents a review of your organization's exciting new direction.

The Art of Collaboration

It's not just about delivering quantifiable performance results that'll keep your stakeholders firmly on your team. You must also assure qualitative success—and that is best provided by collaborative efforts that galvanize community participation and keep everyone marching to the same DMO drummer.

Is one of your core strategies collaborating with local tourism partners to achieve success? For some DMOs, it's just an afterthought.

It's not always on the front burner of need amidst deadline commitments for ongoing planning and delivery around every corner. So sometimes, asking for insights from stakeholders in planning DMO programs does take a backseat and isn't a management priority.

It just doesn't always seem important—that is, until you conduct a stakeholder assessment and discover just how left out your constituents feel about their lack of a participatory role in your future planning and their industry of tourism.

Take a moment and answer this question honestly:

Do you believe a collaborative DMO effort is a good thing?

Most would say, yes, for so many occasions. After all, collaboration builds team support and spirit, leverages resources, and delivers stronger results for the DMO and the destination.

If that's the case, then answer these questions:

What's the difference between input and feedback?

Does your staff understand the difference as well?

If everyone did, I don't think anyone would ever ask for program feedback. Here's why:

- **Input defines what you receive on the front-end** from collaborative stakeholder programs that build consensus and collaboration. It's most often meaningful and actionable.
- **Feedback is back-end**. It's what some ask for after the project has been completed. And what is that worth to your program when you didn't have the foresight to ask for advice and opinions during the project's planning stage? Not much.

Feedback responses are usually half-hearted and mostly meaningless. And the word *meaningless* will likely also describe how your request for feedback is perceived by stakeholders—particularly since the project has now been concluded and offers little to no opportunity for modifications based on stakeholder feedback.

Make a list of the opportunities for gaining important input and building collaboration through partnership efforts, such as the following:

- annual marketing plan development
- strategic planning
- task force and committee assignments
- tourism product development issues for advocacy
- PR roundtable discussions and planning
- convention team selling.

A Collaboration Case Study

One of my favorite collaborative opportunities for producing DMO input is provided every year by CEO Rob Varley's Florida Space Coast Office of Tourism.

Known as Camp Creative, it's a planning session for principal partners who gather in a major meeting room for this popular program.

As tourism stakeholders enter the meeting, there's a feeling of positive energy, with people milling around, getting coffee, and preparing for the session ahead. The room is festively decorated with balloons and banners, and you get the impression that something important will get done here today that is going to be fun, too.

Across the entire room, leadership has set up dozens of tables of ten—each with a center stanchion featuring a hand-printed topic for each table: THE INTERNET, NEW SALES TECHNIQUES, SOCIAL MEDIA, VISITOR SERVICES, ADVERTISING, MEDIA PUBLICITY, and on and on.

More attendees show up, and everyone surveys the room and the topics to be addressed. Then all take their seats until most of the tables are full.

There are still some tables available that don't feature completed signs and discussion topics, but they are soon added by the participants, as other groups join up to work together on recommending other creative approaches for tourism office success.

Now the room is a buzz of conversations, as some participants jump from table to table to provide more input.

Then the session comes to a rousing conclusion over lunch, as a chosen presenter from each table goes to the lectern to announce and describe their table's marketing recommendations.

What follows is robust applause from all participants as the session ends on a high note. Then, in just a few days, the tourism office staff has memorialized the Camp Creative work session in writing and disseminates the new plans with all stakeholders as it begins to tackle the list of great ideas that have been produced.

Wow. What an invigorating program, and what a terrific collaborative DMO effort.

Getting Input from Staff

During an upcoming staff meeting of your organization, I recommend you brainstorm staff suggestions for new opportunities in receiving stakeholder input. And speaking of staff, when was the last time you formally considered what kind of new inputs you personally need from them to round out your own management thinking and performance planning for the future?

Maybe it'll turn out to be another Camp Creative moment—providing a productive step for everyone through the new and ever-evolving art of collaboration.

Product Development

More than ever, destination marketing organizations are applying strategic planning focus for product development and advocacy that can provide leadership in enhancing and revitalizing their communities for tomorrow's traveler.

"One of the common failures of urban planning is a tendency to overlook tourism infrastructure needs and opportunities," cautioned industry consultant expert Jeff Sanford, former chair of the International Downtown Association. "The result is a measurable loss in economic growth—at a time when most municipalities can ill afford to lose anything. For the good of the community, the tourism industry must be a partner in the planning process," Sanford urged.

Destination product development is really all about producing financial performance, economic impact, and market share for your destination. That's why more DMOs are pushing the envelope and taking the next operational step to assure their mission's success through catalytic infrastructure development and other issues of advocacy.

Perhaps you have a perceived need for a conference center, a convention center headquarters hotel, a major new attraction, performing arts center—even just way-finding and pedestrian signage or welcome center programs that can synergistically boost tourism.

Whatever the need, if you're seriously interested in actively providing leadership in supporting the development of new infrastructure development in your community, here are some initial steps that will provide guidance in getting started:

- **Formalize your DMO's interest and commitment to destination development.** You can do this best by first receiving buy-in commitment from your board and memorializing it in a written objective that helps fulfill your mission statement. Hopefully, you've already annunciated your organization's principal objectives that support your mission, including creating customer awareness and interest, increasing visitor length of stay, producing stakeholder partnerships, and providing a research base for industry analysis. Now, add this objective:

To support destination infrastructure development for the community that generates new visitation and resulting benefits for all residents.

- **Ask appropriate government and industry leaders for a "seat**

at the table" for your DMO. After all, you are certainly one of the community's major stakeholders and it's really critical that you proactively have such an ongoing presence for community destination development. For example, if your city is planning a signage program, your unique perspectives for the visitor and your business stakeholders will be critical to the program's success because you best understand your customer's needs, particularly the first-timers; from way-finding signage to welcome center visitor orientation to brochure information, you know the informational and motivational requirements for visitors that signage must support and help fulfill. That is just one example of what you offer and why you consistently need to be in the room for these development discussions and decision making.

- **Be equipped to offer counsel and direction about optimum methods for producing future initiatives.** It's not enough just to have that seat at the table. Sometimes government will create special advisory committees or task forces for project development. That's fine—but when these citizen groups become the end-all in the process, it can sometimes quickly go off track and end up becoming a disaster.

For example, one city mayor appointed a local committee to evaluate and make recommendations on a proposed location for the city's professional baseball park. Discussions by the well-intentioned but unschooled committee members languished so long that the current team left the city, and no formalized recommendation was made that carried the weight of professional assessment. Since then, the mayor has left office and the city's replacement team has dropped from AAA to AA status.

Nearly a thousand miles away, another community appointed a well-meaning committee—this time to assess new uses for a former arena facility. That was five years ago, and little progress has yet to be made.

In both of these situations, there was no traditional master planning, no reliable pro-formas, and no guidance from industry experts who do this work for a living every day. This may be where you come in—advising city leaders about current best practices for destination product development, so you should prepare yourself by understanding the various programs and processes now at work for community product development that can reliably deliver new visitors and produce positive ROIs.

Destination Master Planning

Three exceptional case histories are found in San Antonio, Kansas City, and Oklahoma City, where CSL International of Minnesota has helped change the landscape of destination planning. For background, Conventions, Sports and Leisure International, with more than five hundred assignments, specializes in destination planning and related convention, sports, entertainment, and visitor industry development.

Destination Master Plans

The San Antonio Destination Master Plan

This master plan was intended to provide the community with strategies to (1) enhance the attractiveness of the destination for visitors and residents, (2) protect and enhance the unique cultural and historical visitor industry infrastructure of the destination, and (3) enhance the ability of the visitor industry to create significant economic benefits for the residents of San Antonio.

The planning and research efforts for this destination assignment went well beyond a traditional master planning approach. The final planning document, titled "Destination SA," served as a vehicle for visitor industry input into many traditional tourism planning issues, as well as issues that included River Walk planning, city beautification, downtown retail and housing development, resolutions for traffic and parking issues, park planning, historic preservation, and related issues that have a very important direct or indirect bearing on the visitor industry.

The Kansas City Destination Master Plan

This master plan was focused on many areas including transportation linkages between visitor industry assets, the creation of large-scale public art and landscaping within key visitor industry districts, organizational structure and policy changes for management of key historical and entertainment districts, and policy changes to assist local unique and authentic projects and entrepreneurs.

In addition, extensive convention center planning research was conducted to address market demand, facility and community needs, and financial and economic issues regarding future center enhancements.

The Oklahoma City Destination Master Plan

This master plan emphasized infusing the visitor industry infrastructure with elements that are unique and authentic to Oklahoma City, while protecting the attraction elements already existing there.

Final initiatives may include development of new attractions, long-range convention and exposition center planning, support for hotel development, creating appealing linkages among various visitor zones within the community, and creating policies that encourage visitor industry growth.

Community Infrastructure

To get started in developing community infrastructure, familiarize yourself with the various processes for assessing and planning the development of other specific infrastructure development, including conference centers, convention center hotel development, attractions, and other public assembly facilities.

John Kaatz, principal of CSL International, said that the main priority is to develop a comprehensive community assessment for product differentiation and infrastructure analysis. Its purpose:

To evaluate existing visitor industry infrastructure and amenities and evaluate specific opportunities for enhancements that could serve to improve your destination appeal and drive new visitation.

The process includes market research, industry benchmarking, and case studies of comparable destinations.

The focus is on the following:

- evaluating current conditions that may be hindering the growth of the visitor industry in the destination
- reviewing various need areas for the visitor industry including event facilities, attractions, festivals, and other demand generators (The focus can extend to shortcomings that may not be directly related to the visitor industry such as downtown housing, retail, sidewalk conditions, and public transportation issues.)
- maintaining a focus on elements of the destination that are unique and authentic that can help create differentiation amongst competitive markets
- making sure that the ultimate plan has full buy-in from public sector staff and elected officials, as well as key stakeholders in the visitor industry.

As noted earlier, issues addressed in this analysis could include, but are not limited to, the following:

- Identify lodging infrastructure, existing convention, conference and meeting facilities, and physical improvements that would enhance a visitor-friendly image—including issues such as signage, landscaping, security, aesthetics, green space, transportation linkages, and related features.

- Identify potential support for major destination attractions that could be developed to drive large increases in visitation.
- Evaluate municipal policies and procedures for their effectiveness in supporting the visitor industry—with recommendations designed to encourage visitor-related development.
- Evaluate the adequacy of destination marketing financial resources.
- Identify potential land acquisition needs and funding sources to ensure future visitor industry infrastructure development.
- Identify public sector initiatives that enhance the attractiveness of the destination.
- Clarify the economic impacts from major development opportunities, and include pro-formas as well.
- Evaluate local visitor industry organizations to ensure that the internal structures and cross-organizational linkages are conducive to growing the industry.
- Evaluate how current visitors to the area perceive the destination (through strategic plan findings and additional interviews conducted for this component of work), and identify changes that may be necessary to motivate and deliver additional visitors.
- Assess how regional travelers who have not been to the destination perceive it.

The result of these efforts, along with a comprehensive benchmarking analysis of competitive destinations, will identify strengths and weaknesses of the broad visitor industry, give you detailed strategies for improvement, and roles/responsibilities for particular entities in implementing the recommendations.

For additional information, contact John Kaatz, principal, CSL International, at jkaatz@cslintl.com.

A White Paper Process for Advocacy Issues

What is a white paper? It is an authoritative report or guide that often addresses issues and how to solve them. Although I've not seen many white papers used for framing DMO issues of advocacy, they are quite appropriate.

Traditionally, white papers are used to educate readers and help people make decisions. They're often used in politics, business, and technical fields. In commercial use, the white paper is also employed by businesses as a marketing or sales tool.

The more historical use of the term *white paper* refers to a government-produced document or report. Most commonly, it describes a report made by a governmental agency endorsing a specific policy. These are usually heavily referenced documents that explain research or arguments on a specific issue and then lay out a plan of action. A white paper, when used by the government, may be a precursor to passing or creating a new law.

Today, the corporate or marketing white paper has become much more common. In fact, producing a white paper for the purpose of marketing is now a recognized and accepted marketing tool, many times developed to influence favorable opinion in solving challenges, drawing investors, or creating sales.

In these cases, it may be employed to influence people's opinions about an emerging problem and offer solutions, or it may be used to detail a new technology, service, or product.

Some may discern the latter concept as a sales tactic in disguise. In that case, while the white paper may read like a scientific report with a lot of references and erudition, it is usually meant to generate interest in a particular position or to promote investment or sales of a particular product. It takes skill to craft a document of this type because it is most successful when it doesn't appear to be a commercial sales tactic.

One of the famous writings on how to write a white paper is an easily Internet-accessed essay by Michael Stelzner, "How to Write a White Paper—A White Paper on White Papers." He focuses on the successful elements of the marketing white paper:

- outlining a problem
- evaluating the historical background of a problem
- offering generic concepts that might pose a solution and the benefits
- introducing the unique solution to the problem or writing about the product or idea that will solve the problem.

You can reliably employ this white-paper approach in advocating for a new convention center, a headquarters hotel, downtown master planning, other infrastructural issues, and even new funding requirements.

Why Hire Business Consultants?

This isn't a personal plug for business. It's an explanation of the core reason you will occasionally need outside strategic guidance and support that can assure staff and organizational competitiveness.

I received a call from a DMO executive who was considering hiring me for a quick tune-up of his organization's marketing performance efforts.

"How much do you charge?" he asked.

I told him my standard fee for the week's assignment would be $10,000, plus agreed-to actual expenses forecast in advance. There was a long pause, so I then suggested he might be able to short-circuit the administrative process by considering a sole source contract based on skill sets, and also this wasn't going to take long or cost a lot.

"Um . . . actually . . . I hadn't planned to pay . . . quite that much," he said.

"Have you ever heard of the famous Wyeth family of artists?" I asked the DMO executive.

"Vaguely," he said, "Why?"

"Well, a few years ago, Andrew Wyeth painted a portrait of a man who liked his portrait very much, but he just wasn't happy with the cost. So he asked his attorney to please try to negotiate a better price. 'How long did it take you to paint that portrait of my client?' the attorney asked. Wyeth responded, 'All my life.'"

And then I said to my perspective employer, "Bill, I've also been preparing for your marketing assignment all my life, so to speak, and if you decide to hire me, I will most likely save you more money in less than an hour than the total cost of our potential work together."

The following week I was hired, and the client was very pleased with the results.

Why Should You Hire Business Consultants?

In most cases, appropriate consultants are engaged simply because of their sheer depth of core business competencies and experiences that your staff doesn't yet share—particularly for start-up program development, as well as having many years of success and friendships cultivated with travel intermediaries like writers/ editors, meeting planners, or tour operators—the important people you always need to help market your destination.

For example, if you're starting up a new website, you need an Internet marketing expert to support your Internet staffer in developing the optimum structure and benefits to be accrued.

A new and comprehensive media publicity program requires a strategic planning process from PR communications experts that shows you what it will cost and what it will deliver. And dependent on long-term need, you may later decide to hire outside PR counsel because of their track record in dealing effectively with travel writers who know and respect them and those clients they represent.

In both cases, after the assignment you'll have cultivated an industry expert, as well as a new friend, who now understands the inner workings of your organization and its needs and who will be available for your long-term questions and ongoing support. That can end up being worth a lot to you.

The Recommended Selection Process

For these and most other potential situations like them, you should initiate a competitive request for the proposal process that includes a response to you that provides the cost–benefit relationships in working with these independent business sources. Also, check their references and ask for their past case histories of assignments that parallel your needs.

CHAPTER 3
Customer Sales and Service

"Quality in a service or product is not what you put into it. It is what the client or customer gets out of it."
                                        –Peter Drucker

The Sales Call

It may come as a surprise, but the sales call—the most important marketing tool for maximizing visitor business—is underrated and under-utilized by many organizations.

The DMO sales call reminds me of *The Little Engine That Could*, that industrious little hero in the book that taught children the value of optimism and hard work. But for many organizations today, the sales call initiative is surprisingly missing in action.

At least that's the case for many destination programs where interfacing with the important travel intermediaries of the business—particularly meeting planners, tour operators, and travel writers—has lost a much-needed priority.

Why, you should ask? After all, DMOs are market-driven and customer-focused organizations. But perhaps the sales call is not considered as sexy or glamorous compared to other ongoing initiatives. It's also a labor-intensive process that requires discipline.

The reality is that the sales call is an indispensible priority for your work; it is the foundation for building productive relationships with travel intermediaries.

First, let's take a look at each of these three market segments and address core needs for consideration.

1. The Convention Sales Call

Here in convention sales is where your sales staff should be the most grounded in the discipline of sales call/solicitation.

Sales executives learned early that if they delivered more sales call activity and had productive contacts with meeting planners—and metaphorically put these calls in the marketing funnel—then from the bottom end of the funnel would correspondingly pour out more productivity in the way of planner interest in the destination, sales leads, site inspections, and bid proposals, and ultimately higher volumes of booked business. But even here in convention sales, there's work to be done.

I was once retained to produce a more effective sales plan for a destination convention sales program. After a diagnostics review of its processes and results, it became clear that the sales staff wasn't meeting generally acceptable numbers of required daily calls—either on the phone or through outside office personal calls.

The good news was that the conversion rate of sales leads to business booked was quite effective.

Through individual and group discussions with the sales team, we quickly determined that some functional areas needed to be addressed including team-sell opportunities with hotel stakeholders, sales training for overcoming customer objections, and the realignment of markets among the staff based on skill sets and performance parameters.

But the bottom-line result was that everyone agreed that through some simple reprioritizing of work, it would be feasible for each sales person to increase calls and resulting business by up to 25 percent. Since this approach was implemented, it has stimulated some terrific results for the staff, while also enhancing team morale and a can-do spirit for the staff and its stakeholders.

2. The Tour Operator Sales Call

In this market segment, we begin to generally see less effective use of the sales call—or for that matter, lack of consistent follow-up personal communication intended to confirm the actual booking of tour business that came from a DMO-issued sales lead.

When staff is asked why they can't confirm business that may have been secured by local hotel properties through DMO leads, the answer is sometimes, "well, we asked the properties how they did, but they're reluctant to share that proprietary information with us." That's understandable—and it's also the core reason why the DMO tour sales person should instead be posing this question to the tour operator and not the hotelier.

After all, you assisted the operator in developing the business, and now most will be more than happy to return the favor by quantifying the value of that business and where it is housed. And without these measures of productive performance results, there is really no perceived value for the DMO from this new tour operator business, is there?

We are also occasionally told that the staffer has other commitments that prevent or limit ongoing sales call activity. In that case, the priorities are clearly wrong.

Again, personal contact and support for the DMO client builds a bond for the destination that is not provided solely by written correspondence or through brief sales sessions with operators at national or regional trade shows.

3. The Travel Writer Sales Call

Next, we come to the most significant void for DMO sales calls: the media publicity opportunity afforded by conversations and follow-up with the travel writer fraternity.

If asked, many PR staffers will often share how busy they already are in preparing and disseminating press releases, gathering information for writer requests, hosting on-site writers, and other activities. But those are ancillary, supportive considerations compared to the inherent value of the ongoing writer sales call.

We queried a cross-section of travel writers and media publicity DMO personnel about this issue. Both groups confirmed that the personal sales call to writers is vastly underused—and what a mistake that is, because it is through conversations with writers that the DMO media specialist can quickly

- determine the writer's knowledge and interest in the destination
- get to know the writer on a more personal level
- provide new information for the writer and add the writer to the arsenal of DMO media services for future cultivation
- consider site inspections or group familiarization opportunities for appropriate writers.

First, let's do the math. There are currently about 550 active professional members of the Society of American Travel Writers (SATW). They include many of the top media people that your PR staff should be personally conversing with and getting to know—and not just through press releases or by website support. They include freelancers, travel editors, staff writers, photographers, and TV and radio journalists.

By making just four completed telephone calls daily, your media staffer could be reaching twenty of these writers a week, eighty a month, and every single SATW writer in about seven months. Add to that the important regional media located within a three hundred-mile radius of your destination, and you can efficiently communicate with and influence your entire primary market of media opportunity in less than twelve months. That cycle of ongoing calls should also be continuous.

The result will be far greater awareness, interest, and potential coverage for your destination than is currently being produced.

Planning Recommendations

Managing the success of this new sales work requires

- **an ongoing staff commitment** (I recommend the specific inclusion of a quantified number of ongoing sales calls as part of the formalized job description and personal performance objectives.)
- **development of a comprehensive tracking system** to confirm the categories and results for sales calls made that address each market segment.

Then, as more calls are put into the marketing funnel, you'll begin to notice increases in productive staff results including booked meetings business, tour bookings, and media publicity.

Costs Are Low, Results High

To round out your performance-based program, all it takes is a little advance market planning plus a renewed commitment to this strategically important, yet underutilized sales call initiative.

Postscript

I'm still thinking about that courageous little train engine that accomplished such big dreams. At the time of the story's writing, some critics actually considered it a metaphor for the American dream.

The story of that little engine has been told and retold for the past one hundred years. The underlying theme is the same: a stranded train is unable to find an engine willing to take it over difficult terrain to its destination on the other side of the mountain. Only the little blue engine is willing to try and, while repeating the mantra, "I think I can, I think I can," overcomes a seemingly impossible task.

That's what a lot of DMOs attempt to do every day with finite resources, but with a spirit of belief in the important work they accomplish. I hope your organization is one of them.

Enhancing Your Community's Convention Product

Is your convention product/destination the best it can be? Are you delivering with one voice—and through one seamless convention development program—fulfillment of customer needs through excellent sales and service?

The destination operational models throughout the industry for convention marketing, sales, and service are certainly diverse. In most, however, the center manages its facility as a loss leader, reserving its prime dates for conventions that host visitor delegates who will produce optimal economic impact to the area through room-night generation. And the CVB primarily serves as the community's marketing arm to deliver this critically important business.

The roles can get murky with so many players involved—hotels, restaurants, transportation companies, the center, CVB, etc. Who is ultimately responsible for delivering and monitoring customer service and making sure that the community consistently delivers the highest performance of sales/service results?

From where you sit, you most certainly will say it's the CVB. And while most would agree, the task just can't be efficiently accomplished without a conscious collaborative effort to deliver a seamless program throughout the entire area and convention industry.

Evaluating Customer Service

Step one in enhancing a seamless program is for the community to assess and then work to consistently improve its sales and service efforts.

For service enhancement, secret shopper programs can be effective. So can independent third-party surveys of customers. But one of your most important ongoing tactics should be a fully coordinated service evaluation of the meeting planner following a successful meeting in your city. Sounds reasonable, doesn't it? But you'd be surprised how few are actually being effectively delivered in most communities.

Even when the CVB's convention services coordinator has responsibility for managing this service program, many collect only two to four surveys from every ten meeting planners.

With that poor rate of return, you can't accurately project and evaluate community service. Why does this happen? One consistent excuse is that "the meeting planners didn't focus on answering our questionnaire because they were too busy packing up and getting out of town."

This scenario is just not acceptable in today's business environment. To get to the real reason, go to the job description of the convention services coordinator. Under personal performance objectives, it should state that this person is responsible for delivering the evaluation program—and that requires diligence in retrieving this information from the meeting planner. In fact, the employee's salary compensation should be tied to this important deliverable.

The coordinator must assume and more effectively manage this responsibility. Perhaps an electronic survey will work. Timing the request for the planner to obtain this needed information may be a special consideration. In all cases, a new implementation program should be developed that guarantees ongoing planner input.

As part of the evaluation questionnaire, you should also

- **use a broad one to five grading system** (with one being poor and five excellent) to assess various areas of interest
- **incorporate a follow-up requirement** when service falls in the bottom one to two result areas (In other words, send the questionnaire to deficiently evaluated hotels—but don't stop there; also ask for a copy of their response to the customer.)
- **share your ongoing results with your board** and provide an annual service report to participants as well (This is an important program and should be given ongoing visibility with your leadership.)
- **combine your questionnaire with that of the convention center** where feasible. (It'll enhance your seamless effort and make it easier for response from the meeting planner.)

Developing a New Marketing Agreement

An important process for delivering a seamless sales and service program is through a new marketing agreement with the convention center. The objectives are to enhance communication and accountability, build the team effort, and address the mutuality of your missions.

An annual agreement should list supportive requirements of work delivery for both the bureau and the center. It may include the following:

Collective Commitments

- Develop joint goals for bookings, room nights, space, and revenue.
- Management meets together on a monthly basis to review collective plans, progress, and problems.
- Review and confirm agreement on the standardized definitions of business performance in accordance with the standards of the Destination Marketing Association International, including confirmed bookings, lost business, and canceled business.

CVB Commitments

- Pro-actively promote the convention center in all selling activities.
- Attend weekly (monthly or quarterly) joint sales meetings.
- Partner with the sales and executive staff for customer events.
- Conduct joint site inspections with all customers.
- Block all meeting and exhibit space accurately.
- Provide history and RFP for meetings and conventions (when appropriate).
- Maximize the use of the exhibit and meeting space at the convention center for meetings and trade shows.
- Develop a new-hire cross-training program for convention center sales staff.
- Deliver a year-end report for the convention center board that reviews past year CVB bookings of meetings for the future, including meeting space, hotel room nights produced, estimated economic impact to the community, and forecasts the booking goals for the coming year.

Convention Center Commitments

- Make available a perpetual five-year future grid for the building to share with the bureau. Attend all weekly/quarterly sales meetings of the bureau.
- Quote competitive pricing.
- Attend trade shows with bureau when appropriate (identify all).
- Provide tours and related food and beverage during bureau-sponsored FAM/site trips.
- Partner with the bureau during all sales missions.
- Partner with the bureau during all customer events.
- Make effort to work with bureau's sales managers to accommodate short-term bookings within the agreed-upon timeframe.
- Develop a new-hire cross-training program for bureau sales staff.
- Deliver a year-end report for the CVB's board to review the year's joint efforts.

Other Seamless Program Opportunities

Now that you're on your way to producing this seamless new program, also consider other opportunities:

- **Jointly review the 2007 Report on Best Practices** for Convention Center Sales and Convention Center Operations from the DMAI-IAVM (Int. Assn. of Venue Managers) Joint Study Committee.

- **Develop an integrated center/CVB team-sell approach** that requires joint sales team members to call on customers together (and with hotel sales execs on board as part of this team-sell approach, too).
- **Deliver an ongoing sales training program** for the center, bureau, and participating hotels—new training for all three collective partners should be developed. Training topics should include team selling, overcoming customer objections, and telemarketing sales techniques.
- **Consider placing at least one seasoned CVB sales executive** in the center—with exclusive responsibility for center/citywide business solicitation—a model that has received high marks for its seamless, performance-based functionality.

Finally, because this is an annual agreement, take the opportunity of formally reviewing it every year with the intention of providing continuous and never-ending improvement to the process.

Why Do You Lose Convention Business to Other Communities?

Who's taking it away, and what can you do to get it back?

The following issues help diagnose and resolve community lost convention business.

Issue 1: Lost Convention Business

Just about every CVB produces versions of lost business reports as a method for determining the reasons why business has not been achieved from potential clients.

It's a standard requirement for sales managers to query meeting planners following the unsuccessful competitive bid proposal process. The CVB sales supervisor asks for the completed lost business report, but in some cases today, the process used does not effectively provide the detailed answers that could help achieve greater future performance success.

What we really need to know from the lost business report are answers to the following questions:

- On an ongoing basis, what are the primary reasons we consistently lose business to other communities?
- To whom do we lose it?
- Are there major competitors who consistently win out against us?
- What are the reasons for our competitor's success and for our resulting failure to achieve these bookings?

Can you supply these answers through your lost business reports? If not, you're simply not deploying the correct report process for discovery and analysis— and you are handicapping yourself for future successful market planning.

Going forward, each lost business report should include

- the number of requested rooms, potential attendance, and total estimated economic impact
- the competitive city or facility who won the business
- the reason why the destination lost the business.

I have seen some unsatisfactory reports that simply concluded, "lost to another city." Instead, offer a detailed list of potential and specific reasons for consideration, and then add to them with further input from planners. Your initial list may include the following reasons:

- climate
- competitor's pricing (fair market value)
- convention center rates too high
- center dates not available
- hotel dates not available
- inadequate booking policy
- geographic rotation
- hotel rates too high
- inadequate exhibit space
- inadequate meeting space
- inadequate meeting space at hotel
- inadequate number of rooms at hotel
- lack of client response
- lack of headquarters hotel
- lack of hotel response
- lack of local support
- lack of union facilities
- overall pricing too high
- politics of group
- preferred dates not available
- quality of service
- requires larger hotel(s)
- turned away to accommodate better business.

Now you're ready to deliver the strategic assessment of where your community is in relationship to the competition.

By taking all of your individual lost business reports throughout the year and incorporating them in one comprehensive annual analysis through your customer relationship management program, you can determine, on a percentage basis, the primary reasons for your annual losses—and begin to do something about it.

If, for example, you are challenged by the lack of a headquarters hotel, the annual analysis will also show and value how much business you lose annually because of this liability. And your report will serve as a useful feasibility study resource in support of such a new facility.

If hotel pricing is a dilemma, then you can review this challenge with your accommodations partners. I know hotel communities who were unaware that they were the primary cause for lost convention business, because they hadn't paid special attention to the needs for some judicious rate modification in relationship to their leisure rate—or in modifying the community's window for convention solicitation—and were quick to do so in future partnership with the CVB.

You'll also learn which communities successfully competed and won against your destination. And if you discover that the same competitive cities consistently win out against your ongoing efforts, it's time to undertake a detailed competitive set analysis of these destinations by comparing the following:

- CVB budget and staffing, field offices, sales initiatives deployed
- special marketing programs and considerations for convention development
- infrastructure advantages (convention center, ballroom, location, other facilities)
- financial package support.

Issue 2: Why Many Convention Cities Are Selected

Ongoing market research conducted throughout the North American meetings industry has consistently concluded that major convention planners rank the following destination attributes high on their list of requirements:

- convenient destination location / ease of accessibility
- favorable pricing and date availability
- convention center space and service ability
- convenient proximity of hotels to meeting facilities.

There are also secondary, supportive needs that may include among others

- shuttle service and other convention services: welcoming programs, media attention, pre- and post-meeting opportunities
- spouse programs
- nearby shopping, restaurants, attractions, tour options, and entertainment
- language translation services, currency exchange, international signage when required.

However, when meeting planners were asked, "What is the number-one reason a particular destination was ultimately chosen for a meeting?" The answer was universally:

The destination itself

What does this really mean? It confirms that planners principally choose meeting destinations (after they are comfortable that adequate convention requirements are available) based on the unique appeals of the particular destination: the community's personality, culture, heritage, or inherent qualities that separate it from other communities in the eyes of their attendees.

Thus, when attempting to positively influence the meeting planner's decision-making process, the DMO should:

Wrap its convention product positioning and its meeting "hardware" with its compelling leisure tourism personality and benefits

This approach shows up frequently today in successful convention ad campaigns, on websites, and in trade show exhibits. It's an opportunity that you should consistently emulate if your destination brand is considered sufficient to the task.

The Emerging Trend for Convention Solicitation

I have begun to refer to this trend as the "show me the money" syndrome.

It occurs primarily at the convergence of any number of market conditions: a sagging economy, the consolidation or reduction in meetings and convention delegate attendance, lower hotel occupancy and less room nights filled, the emergence of new competitive DMOs, new or expanded national and regional convention center product, and the tightening budget requirements of association meetings.

Here's one recent and quite dramatic example. A meeting planner for a California state association was preparing to select a major city within the state for its next annual meeting when he received an unexpected phone call from a sales executive at a top Las Vegas hotel property on the Strip.

"We just heard about your next meeting and would very much like to make you an offer if we're not too late," the Vegas sales executive said.

"Well, what's your proposal?" asked the California meeting planner.

"Free," was the quick, succinct response.

"Free what?"

"Free welcoming reception. Free meals. Free conference rental space. And free delegate accommodations. In other words, free convention," the sales executive said. "Your association matches the gaming profile of our customer," he explained, "and we would really love to host you next year." And, as they say, that was that.

While the above is certainly not illustrative of the norm in requirements for convention support, issues like this are becoming more prevalent. And there's little doubt that deeper discounting is the requirement in today's increasingly competitive meeting business. For example, many major convention and tradeshow events are now requiring at least a 50 percent discount of convention center rental—and this reality has forced many destinations to provide meeting incentives.

Therefore, it makes business sense for DMOs to formally create a Convention Development Fund that would apply ongoing available resources to help book new business, offsetting required costs for conventions having the greatest potential for achieving high economic impact returns to the community.

A partnership approach with the convention center would be an optimum arrangement. So is the continuation of hotel rebate programs. DMO sales managers would make recommendations for priority use for the convention development fund based on economic generation from the business, and monies would then be escrowed until required during the year for hosting.

A Convention Sales Case Study

Boosting convention sales performance was the objective when we were retained by a popular historic destination that had many convention attributes but only modest production results.

Following a comprehensive on-site situation analysis including reviews of lost business, current sales processes, and marketing initiatives from CVB and hotel sales executives, we produced a new, integrated sales and general marketing plan highlighted by more than twenty major marketing and operational recommendations, including

- **realignment of existing and new sales personnel**, deploying the top CVB staff producers based on their expertise and actual results, with a new concentration on citywide business skewed to larger attendance and having higher demographic characteristics
- **development of new team-sell training programs** for hotel, center, and CVB personnel, concentrating on team sales strategies and techniques for overcoming customer objections
- **increased the goal of completing 25 percent more annual staff sales calls**, which alone was responsible for closing about 25 percent more annual convention business and room night generation
- **strengthened the community's team-sell plan** for hotel/ convention center/CVB execs by tripling the number of team calls made during ongoing trade shows, sales blitzes, and other forums, while adding a new and expanded program of seasonal follow-up familiarization programs for meeting planners.

With full endorsement by the CVB and its principal stakeholders, the plan provided an opportunity for the community to generate the following future results:

- **an annual 40 to 50 percent potential increase** in total annual bookings, amounting to 20,000–25,000 new room nights and yielding about eight to ten annual new conventions

- **an additional estimated $7 million to $8.75 million** in resulting new annual visitor impacts to the community's economy from booked conventions
- **up to an additional fifty event days** to the convention center, while producing an estimated $780,000 in new center revenue.

Developing Destination Market Expansion through Product Diversification

"Will the last person out of town please turn off the lights," was the public concern about Atlantic City's decaying future prior to its Phoenix-like rise beginning in the late 1970s as the East Coast's new casino gaming capital. But even then, government and business leadership knew they had much more to do if they were going to effectively compete in the tourism marketplace.

How does a one-trick pony destination like a gaming capital grow and flourish? Through product enhancement, diversification of the visitor market, and a focused new and aggressive marketing program.

Atlantic City's plans included

- **a casino industry that could produce new tax revenue** that was reinvested in infrastructure like new housing and new beautification projects including a Grand Boulevard city gateway, hospitals, schools, visitor services, and other amenities, highlighted by new casino hotel room expansion
- **new state government authorities to manage and oversee** this critically important work, including

  - the Casino Reinvestment Development Agency for the above tasks
  - the Casino Control Commission to assure legal and fiduciary compliance of casino management operations
  - the Convention and Visitors Authority, which I was hired to develop and manage. The principal task: to merge operations of the old convention center with the existing CVB to form this Authority. At the top of the list of opportunities was market diversification and new economic impact returns to be provided by a new $275 million convention center that could effectively compete with the mature Northeast US convention marketplace.

"The New Atlantic City: We're betting a billion on it!" was the scary CVB advertising headline that initially heralded this new and positive future. I suspect that few people at the time were certain this could become a credible, deliverable promise. (After all, destinations are supposed to guarantee a great visitor experience—not place a wager on it.)

By the time I arrived in 1994, construction for the new convention center was underway and slated for opening three short years later. Unfortunately, future business meetings for the new building was on a no-growth path—primarily because of the sagging reputation of the existing old center constructed nearly seventy years earlier, due to its deteriorating condition, limited size, operational challenges, and not-so-stellar service.

Would there be enough consumer confidence and related convention bookings to prevent the new convention center from becoming a big white elephant for Atlantic City and New Jersey? There was a lot of negative press to overcome. Casinos also expressed varied degrees of reluctance in blocking overnight room nights for meeting delegates at the expense of their traditional gaming customers.

Program Milestones

- **DMO board members** were asked to take a strong, effective role in telling Atlantic City's new story along with our staff— and they responded on the road with persuasive appearances at national convention trade shows and sales forums.

- **We ramped up frequent "hard hat" familiarization tours** and site inspections for steady streams of convention and trade show planners, as well as for the media—and again board members added street-credibility in communicating and getting to know future clients and customers. Hundreds of meeting planners were targeted and gladly came for this show-and-tell approach, thanks to our five-star new convention services team that planned and produced some terrific on-site events for customers, including headline shows with such luminaries as Luciano Pavarotti and Tony Bennett and the fun and excitement of the Miss America Pageant.

- **The new Atlantic City convention center** was marketed as "America's New Northeast Business Address," with its more than a half-million feet of contiguous space that covered the footprint of six football fields, the largest configuration of space on one floor from Atlanta through Boston, and America's eleventh largest center featuring the industry's most advanced technology. SMG Management, the top private management firm for public facilities was hired, and that sent a strong signal of professionalism throughout the marketplace.

- **Many casino properties quickly lost their reluctance** to provide needed room blocks for the convention trade when the governor appointed the head of the Casino Control Commission to our board, and pragmatic, acceptable provisions were made with the casinos to support both their traditional gaming casino customer, as well as making room available for the emerging new meetings market delegate.

Tangible Results

When the new convention center and headquarters hotel opened its doors three years later in 1997, it was officially reported that more than 290 future conventions and trade shows had been booked for Atlantic City through 2007.

This was clear testimony to the aggressive work of the staff and the leadership and active support of the board and the power of familiarization programs that introduced a new era of confident new meeting planners and their business to the new Atlantic City.

Customer Service and the Repercussions of Poor Quality Service

Everyone does a lot of talking about customer service. But what is the best model for success? And what happens when you don't follow it?

Kirk Douglas, yesteryear's Hollywood screen star—although better known today as the father-in-law of Welsh actress Catherine Zeta-Jones—tells a story about customer service. During his salad days, Douglas was making the rounds for theater auditions in New York when he stopped for breakfast at a little diner on the lower east side.

"Yeah and wha-da-ya-want?" the hash house waitress grumbled a greeting.

"Just some coffee, toast, scrambled eggs, my dear," Douglas jovially responded, "and a few kind words."

A few minutes later, the waitress returned with his order, plopping the platter down on the Formica table with a clang. As she turned to leave, Douglas asked with a smile, "And where are my few kind words?"

His waitress didn't miss a beat. "Don't eat the eggs," she growled over her shoulder.

Customer service. What's it all really mean these days? And what is expected from the traveler to your community?

Dealing with Customer Expectations

Most focus group research today concludes that it all has to do with the consumers' service expectations—and their belief that the service they deserve away from home while traveling should actually exceed their needs.

The dilemma, therefore, is being able to forecast acceptable levels of customer service on a consistent basis and then deliver it. But there's the rub, because there is really no consistency when addressing the individual traveler's needs. They're all different, with various expectations, diverse wishes, and personal levels of acceptability.

It's a fact, though, that customer problems can mean lost business forever. A much-noted industry survey concludes that 70 percent of all people who experience problems while traveling don't complain. They just walk away—and an alarming 91 percent of them never return nor ever again purchase that travel product or service.

And that's truly alarming, because you'll never know what happened. Think about it. You spent precious marketing dollars getting them there, then wham! They have a problem, they leave, they don't share their concerns with anyone, and they're gone forever.

Validate Your Service

Former New York Mayor Ed Koch used to consistently ask constituents on the subway, "How'm I doing?!" (And believe me, he got an earful every time.) With the mayor's same vigor, we in the travel industry need to establish ongoing ways to consistently validate our daily service with customers.

The simplest and most successful technique is to just ask: Is everything satisfactory? Can I help you with anything? And then your staff must be sufficiently prepared to follow up immediately and make good about whatever needs fixing with their immediate attention.

The King of Customer Service Case Study

In the search for best customer service practices, people have been flocking to Norwalk, Connecticut, for decades to visit Stew Leonard's Dairy Store.

Many come just to tour the store. Others come to attend Stew Leonard University, a two-hour seminar devoted to sharing the dairy store's secrets to its world-famous reputation for high-quality customer service. And in recent years, Leonard's has also taken the story on the road for educational seminars.

Why Stew Leonard's? He may not be your typical guru of customer service, but owner Stew Leonard certainly qualifies as an expert. He's been dedicated to customer service since the day he learned a valuable lesson soon after opening the dairy store in 1969.

Leonard was standing near the front of his store when a woman complained to him that some eggnog he'd sold her tasted sour. Leonard tasted the eggnog, determined that it tasted fresh, and tried to prove to the customer that he was right and she was wrong. Leonard won the argument but lost the customer.

After realizing he had lost a customer over a 99 cent carton of eggnog, Leonard made a public pledge with a 6,000-pound piece of granite and a chisel to put the customer first—always.

Leonard dumped the huge rock at the front of his store. Then he had two rules chiseled into the rock, which have been his motto ever since. At the front of his store, you can still see those two rules engraved in that heavy stone:

Rule number one: The customer is always right.

Rule number two: If the customer is ever wrong, re-read rule number one.

That granite-engraved advice has turned Stew Leonard's into gold. The dairy store has grown from a little seven-item store with seven employees to one that employs seven hundred people, carries eight hundred items, receives nearly one hundred thousand customers a week, and has sales of $100 million a year.

Searching for Customer Service Pledges

Wherever I travel, I'm on the lookout for publicly posted service pledges for the customer. Unfortunately, I don't see very many, and when I do, most of them aren't particularly memorable or credible.

How about you? When was the last time you saw customer service pledges prominently displayed

- in an airport?
- at a visitor welcome center?
- in a restaurant?
- at an attraction?
- at a convention center?

When I was checking into a Radisson Hotel, I received this truly surprising welcome message on a little card with my key:

"OUR GOAL AT RADISSON IS 100% GUEST SATISFACTION"

The pledge continued: "If you are not satisfied with something, please let us know and we'll make it right or you won't pay." I'm really impressed with this offer. It doesn't get any clearer than this.

I also believe that the most effective service pledges are actually written by the employees themselves and not by management.

In Atlantic City, when the new convention center was being completed, the staff developed a new pledge to customer service and had it prominently placed throughout the building for everyone to see. Following the building's opening, customer service evaluations there were consistently higher as compared to other centers.

Put Your Service Focus Center-Stage

Ask yourself if there is a role and new opportunity for your organization in building community business support for an enhanced customer service program throughout the entire area. I'm not referring to secret shopper programs or annual community service awards that you bestow on worthy travel industry employees.

I'm suggesting a new major publicly recognized program that salutes the customer and acknowledges their contributions to our communities. Think about it. Wouldn't that be a novel idea—a DMO that works to develop a positive reputation for its community as one that treats each and every visitor with truly special red carpet service?

There's a unique opportunity here for a community to garner a lot of positive media publicity and consumer attention with such a program.

Striving for Excellence

One morning, I asked our convention center services manager how successful he thought we were, and he confidently replied, "I think we're about 99 percent there."

"Okay," I responded. "But if I equate your 99 percent answer to what's happening everywhere else, that might create a lot of problems about that little one percent service deficiency. For example, it might mean that today a lot of air traffic controllers would send hundreds of planes to the wrong airports, thousands of babies born in hospitals would be delivered to the wrong parents, millions of retirees would get somebody else's social security checks. . . ."

"Oh, okay, all right," he laughed, waving his arms around in mock surrender. "I get your point. We need to strive for 100 percent satisfaction." And that's true. Isn't it?

Keynoting Customer Service

My absolutely all-time favorite customer service story occurred when a national tourism association in New York invited the head of the Canadian Tourist Office to provide the keynote address for its annual meeting.

"I'd be delighted," he agreed, "with one condition. I'd like to choose all those who sit at the head table during my presentation." The meeting sponsors agreed.

When the time came for the opening session, there were ten people sitting at the head table, each one dressed to the nines—yet not a single one of them was recognized by the audience of tourism industry executives.

"Before beginning my remarks today, I am pleased to introduce our distinguished head table," began the Canadian tourism guest speaker. "And as I call their names, I ask each of them to please stand. To my far right and your left, is Mr. David Snider. Mr. Snider was the taxi driver who brought me to the hotel this morning from La Guardia Airport. Next, is Miss Hattie Columbus, who provided maid service for my room today." And so he continued, introducing the bellman, the restaurant waiter, the hotel concierge, the docent at the Metropolitan Museum, until all were standing, smiling broadly, and obviously pleased and proud to be recognized and honored.

"Ladies and gentlemen," the guest speaker gestured dramatically with outstretched hands, "here before you are the excellent tourism industry ambassadors of New York City who personally assisted me today." Then looking toward the mayor who was seated just down front at a table reserved for other dignitaries, he continued, "And you, Mr. Mayor, are certainly vital to this city's wonderful industry of tourism, but not nearly so important to me as these fine ladies and gentlemen who have made my travel stay here in New York so very memorable indeed!"

In quick response, the entire assemblage stood en masse and gave the head table a rewarding and much deserved rousing ovation. It was a truly memorable event.

Publicly Recognize Your Customer Service Ambassadors

Just remember, if it's customer service that we intend to address and enhance, we must first begin by consistently recognizing the value of these service ambassadors and the important work they do.

You should look for new ways to do that through awards, public presentations, and tangible tokens of true appreciation. Maybe a luncheon for their family, tickets to a special event, something truly unexpected but certainly deserved.

For delivering visitor needs, it's simply all about listening to the changing needs and expectations of the customer. If we all did that, we'd chart a much more productive course for destination service success.

The Visitor Welcome Center

Over the years, I've built and managed multiple systems of visitor centers that serviced hundreds of thousands of visitors annually. But I'm still surprised with the answers I sometimes get from center operators.

Try it. Ask the director of a visitor center what its mission is, and they're likely to look at you as if you just fell off a pumpkin truck.

"To welcome visitors, of course," they will usually reply. Or, "to introduce them to the community and its tourism amenities."

If that's the response you get or give, then the visitor center may be your most underrated and undervalued marketing initiative. Well, of course your center is the community's welcome mat for visitors—particularly for first-time visitors. But that's not why you should be spending marketing funds to construct and operate a feel-good service.

No, the bottom-line reason is:

To increase visitor length of stay and resulting dollar expenditures and to encourage repeat visitation that produces additional income to your community.

However, it's not enough to just say it and wish it would happen—you should deliver that promise—then measure and evaluate your ongoing efforts to assure success.

Strangely enough, most destinations don't follow that premise or take the time and effort to nurture and mature the visitor center program.

Instead, they usually welcome visitors with a hello and then either answer a few of their questions or allow visitors to fend for themselves. Then the travelers usually meander about to find brochures or other information and perhaps view an orientation film. Finally, as quickly as they arrived, they disappear.

If that's what's happening at your center, consider this: your information center is your principal contact point with travelers to your destination. Don't miss the opportunity to manage the customer's experience there and build new profits for your community by extending visitor's stay with greater value to the customer, too. And that will go a long way toward encouraging repeat visitation. I'm talking about more unplanned new room night reservations, more tickets to attractions, and more restaurant meals.

Here's how: First, with staff collaboration, begin development of a new or expanded operations manual for all full-time or part-time employees. Staff participants should first produce an introductory section, beginning with the DMO mission statement, which should be followed by a new mission for the visitor center. This sets the stage for a disciplined marketing process for successful operations.

Guidelines for Consideration

Next, staff should work together to expand the following recommendations and objectives for operating the center and fulfilling their operational mission as follows:

- **Capture the traveler's attention**—Say hello, make eye contact, extend a warm, smiling welcome, ask where they're from and if this is their first trip to the area (now you're beginning to build rapport—a needed commodity to get the job done).

- **Give them what they want**—Pull together the experiences and the places they wish to visit. Then it's time to find out how you can really help (not just them, but your DMO and destination). Listen to not only what they say, but also what they don't say. For instance, if they're interested in history and a particular site—perhaps they're also interested in other related places and things to see and do, but they just don't know about them because (as you've just found out) it's their first trip to the area.

- **Emulate the "supermarket" model**—Now that you've found out their principal interests, begin developing an itinerary with what's compatible from the nearby shelf of attractions, that includes more of the same kinds of experiences—and don't forget to make room for lunch and dinner and the array of dining options from which they'll make their personal choices.

- **Learn to read upside down**—That's right. Here, you want to take the customer on a planned adventure by placing an area travel map between you and them. And as you plan and validate their growing interests, you can keep eye contact while introducing your new guests to your destination through a personalized, planned tour route that you've highlighted for them in yellow.

Measuring Success

Now it's time to develop a mechanism for evaluating your center's success in producing increased length of stay, additional room-night generation, and resulting revenue to the community.

This analysis can be provided by a local marketing firm or even initiated as a marketing or research class project by a nearby college or university.

The process involves intercepting travelers after they've exited the center, asking them questions about their initial travel intentions upon arrival, and then after they've received travel counseling from your staff. A postcard or email survey can then be provided for them to fill out and return when they arrive home. And naturally, you'll want to offer an incentive to boost returns.

You'll be amazed at the results: double-digit percentage increases in room-night generation, extended stays, and perceived added value of the customer's visitor experience.

You'll also discover that the more time your counselor spends with each visitor, the longer the duration of their extended trip. So it stands to reason that you'll want to find a method for holding visitors longer in the center—perhaps by allowing them to linger around a well-placed brochure kiosk or by enjoying a visual orientation and soaking up the destination's personality.

And now, the next time you review your marketing efforts for your board or community stakeholders, you'll be able to prominently recognize the efforts of the visitor center staff—and the important payback in ROI that they're providing for your community.

CHAPTER 4
Management and Operations

"Leadership is the ability to produce positive change."
–Lee Iacocca

Today's Successful DMO: Matching the Model

If a tourism destination is to achieve optimum success, an important requisite must be an effective, business-standard destination marketing organization, which, regardless of its size and budget, effectively operates on behalf of the community.

Many will agree that the most effective DMO should deliver a productive marketing program for government, industry, and community residents by enhancing the profit potential of tourism. It also partners to maximize resources and achieve strong performance, ever mindful of tourism's positive impacts for the community in producing new visitor receipts, tax revenue, and jobs generated and sustained through visitor spending, along with the positive social benefits of travel amenities and facilities for the enjoyment of all.

How, then, should we interpret success? What is the profile of today's successful DMO, and how can an organization match its deliverables for business excellence?

The Destination Marketing Association International has provided stellar industry leadership in educational program development for DMOs, including individual professional certification for destination marketing executives (the CDME Program) as well as the accreditation program for DMOs (known as DMAP). They continue to enhance professionalism for the industry through their ongoing program training and educational offerings.

For this profile assessment, there are three major areas or success criteria, which, when taken collectively, provide generally agreed-upon and recognized requisites for evaluating today's successful organization.

Criterion I: Performance Success

The DMO delivers performance of economic development benefits in fulfilling its core mission.

First, its performance results, or economic impacts, are based on the attraction of incremental visitors through various market segments deployed by the staff.

These results are

- quantifiable and including ROI in program costs
- forecast whenever feasible in advance as a series of goals
- reportable to DMO leadership, government, stakeholders, and other community constituents.

In summary, the DMO forecasts its future successful achievements and provides them in advance to its constituent community.

Criterion II: Best Practices for Marketing and Management

The DMO provides marketing, management, and operational excellence through its financial oversight, market research and planning, and introduction of best practices for business execution.

As such, the agency strives to deliver the highest standards of performance in the areas of

- economic performance results against market segments
- successfully planned, designed, and executed marketing initiatives and a business standard marketing plan
- reporting and accountability systems
- short-term and long-term strategic planning
- goal-setting, tracking, and delivery
- staff and program performance evaluation, professional staff development, and employee compensation and recognition
- community partnership and alliance-building to galvanize tourism industry interests, stretch resources, and leverage success.

This is really the core work of the successful DMO under the direction of the president/CEO, and the most well-regarded organizations employ state-of-the-art management systems found throughout the industry.

Criterion III: Community Leadership

The DMO should be the recognized leader in the community for effective tourism development.

Today's DMO should be well regarded for its local leadership position. Government and other major stakeholders (i.e., hotels, attractions, art and cultural institutions, related businesses, and other associations) should look to the DMO as their senior partner and the focal point for destination management and marketing, planning, coordinating community stakeholder efforts, research, and long-range visioning.

Through leadership of the president and board, the DMO's role is that of the voice of the industry, the inspiration, the chief lobbying organization, and the chief advocate for tourism issues—closely monitoring and managing key marketing issues affecting the destination such as the need for competitive market funding, sustainable tourism issues, infrastructure development requirements such as downtown development, lodging accommodations, sports and entertainment facilities, festivals, events and celebrations, along with other visitor amenities and service issues.

Evaluating Success

Methods for evaluating the DMO's performance can be achieved through a combination of processes, including a stakeholder assessment survey of community partners; members and leaders from government and industry; surveys of industry travel intermediaries including meeting planners, travel writers, and tour operators who work with the DMO; and an independent evaluation that includes an objective assessment of organizational management and operational and marketing performance.

A Great Indicator of a Successful DMO

Tampa Bay & Company was voted "Favorite Economic Development Organization" in the first ever *Tampa Bay Business Journal's* Best in the Biz: Readers' Choice Awards.

The process began in early July 2011 when the newspaper began soliciting nominations from readers through an online form in nearly sixty categories focused on business-to-business relationships. Hundreds of nominations were received from all across the paper's seven-county coverage area. Nearly 6,000 people participated in the survey, promoting the process on social media channels and providing discourse and feedback.

Comprised of about seven hundred members, the mission of Tampa Bay & Company is to create vibrant growth for the Tampa Bay area by promoting, developing, and expanding a united visitor industry.

Working with the Media

Nothing can tear down the good work of a DMO faster than ineffective—or nonexistent—media relationship management programs. But community PR isn't about spin-doctoring. It's about building reputation by producing and then communicating successful achievements.

Before entering the tourism industry, I cut my teeth in the field of communications—as a *Fortune* 500 PR practitioner, local county government public information manager, US Naval Public Affairs Officer, and TV news anchor. What I learned then, I've always applied to the daily communications management function of DMOs.

For starters, remember this: the operable word for building PR success for your DMO is based on the positive *reputation* of your organization—and not its *image*. One of your principal objectives will always be fostering community good will, support, and participation in your successful program efforts. With that priority, the media will play an important role in your efforts—and you should have a formal plan to guide direction, just as you do for all other market segments.

We are, after all, in the marketing business of determining customer needs and then trying to best fill those needs, be they from potential visitors, meeting planners, tour operators, travel writers, community stakeholders, etc. Some would also correctly describe that as providing effective public relations or public affairs management.

The Public Affairs Role of DMOs

Most communications experts agree that public relations, or public affairs, should be everybody's job—from the entry-level position to the chairman of the board. Throughout the corporate business community, where stockholders drive the future, public affairs has been elevated to a management role at the senior most executive level. This is certainly an appropriate objective for DMOs, too.

Such a public affairs approach, if properly planned and executed, will foster continued community good will, support, and participation in your agency and its work. Public affairs is, therefore, a planned senior management function that includes

- **initial assessment of stakeholder perceptions** about the agency and its programs
- **a resulting plan of strategic objectives**, strategies, and tactics to produce and enhance public goodwill for the agency
- **ongoing evaluations** to measure this program's continued effectiveness.

Some DMOs may appropriately decide to incorporate this responsibility within the communications function. Others may see it as a stand-alone requirement for CEO leader direction. Others may integrate the role as a performance objective for all senior managers.

Without a doubt, this function is critical to the success of today's DMO, and it should have such a written plan.

Government Interests and the Public's Right to Know

A DMO that receives funds through legislatively dedicated tax revenues is usually viewed by local government as a quasi-government agency—or at least the tax receipts are considered government funds. With that funding relationship comes responsibilities for strong fiduciary and management requirements as well as public accountability and public disclosure.

Some DMOs have been slow to grasp the significance of this understanding, causing strained relationships with government, the local media, and the agency's resulting relevant requirements for program accountability and transparency. Indeed, this can be a source of contention between DMO management, government officials, the media, and the public they serve. It has been cause for at least several major DMO audits.

DMOs also operate in a cultural environment of great complexity. While principally funded by government, they are also usually nonprofit organizations that are established to produce quantifiable, incremental results for the communities and diverse businesses they also serve.

Yet many of the initiatives they must undertake—such as travel for sales, service, and customer hosting and entertainment—can appear lavish in the eyes of the general public or government constituents. This concern usually occurs when there is little backup documentation provided to appropriately justify the expense—particularly direct ROI of expended funds. And indeed, the task of influencing public understanding for the DMO's culture and its resulting work is an ongoing and sometimes daunting one, requiring management dedication to the broader public affairs mission.

Accountability

Also, some community leaders interested in the development of leisure and convention business don't always recognize the significant value of the destination marketing agency or perceive its abilities to actually produce incremental business. In these cases, the DMO has ongoing educational requirements to inform constituents about the processes employed to produce positive economic results from your array of marketing efforts.

Thus, there is a compelling requirement for DMOs who receive public funding by tax revenues or other government/business funding to be fully transparent: consistently publicly accountable for communicating their marketing programs and resulting returns.

As DMO management prepares to make business decisions, any potential public issues should be viewed and evaluated from a public affairs perspective as well as from a legal perspective, weighing the public and media reactions and responses. For example, does your organization have potential public issues or concerns that your governing body would not care to read about on the front page of tomorrow's paper or see reported on the local TV news? If so, additional reflection is required to first craft a communications response to issues before they are acted upon.

If the DMO is not in a position to respond to the media's request for information about a particular issue, it should at least be able to provide a public statement of credible explanation as to why it cannot respond. Otherwise, media officials are likely to view the organization and its actions with mistrust. In these cases, the likely scenario is for the media to use their resources to publicly question the agency's work performance or its public policies.

Government Affairs

To assure a foundation of good government affairs, community officials may sometimes be appointed to the board of the DMO. In some cases, the mayor's or city manager's representative may have a seat on the board or executive committee. In other communities, the top elected official may be deemed the honorary board chairman. In any case, care should be taken to strengthen this critically important government relationship.

Documentation and Transparency

Care should be taken to accurately evaluate the intended purpose of any expense against the DMO's fundamental mission and principal objectives.

For example, in the area of sales, a familiarization program for convention meeting planners that incorporates limousine service, tickets to local entertainment, restaurant meals, and other services should be accompanied by an independent thumbnail analysis of the potential economic benefits that would be derived from the booking of these meetings. This summary would include the number of potential delegates, room nights, and resulting economic impacts to the community. It may also be useful to share the economic impact benefits that were produced as a result of the association's prior annual meeting that was held in one of your competitor's destinations.

We also recommend that government funds be segregated from private sector funding—using private business funding, for example, to pay for travel and entertainment and other programs of potential public sensitivity. But regardless of the source of these funds, if they are perceived as not being appropriately and judiciously expended, the DMO may still find itself in potential conflict with government policy and concern.

Public Affairs

A comprehensive media relations program should be in place to determine in advance what materials, resources, and records from the DMO will be publicly available, along with a comprehensive, proactive media communications program that supports the public affairs agenda of the organization.

Positive media relationships will produce favorable impressions for your agency that enhance its reputation over time. But these efforts must be part of a proactive plan and not initiated after negative coverage has occurred.

The public affairs function is but a part of a major communications program. A program outline follows:

- **Who is assigned the role of media spokesperson** for issues regarding policy, office management, marketing initiatives, and ongoing industry matters? If you relegate that role to your communications department, you're minimizing your importance, visibility, and responsibility as CEO—that responsibility must be vested in you.

- **The best practice** is for the communications department to initially field the request. They should use a media form to document the news inquiry, and then get it to you right away with their recommended input. This way, you can provide the proper attention to your response, delivering the most effective, credible messages. Most problems start when the response is not well thought out to provide the best and most complete answer.

- **Have a written policy for who speaks to the media**; you can't very well manage an effective process if everyone has liberty to publicly speak without a planned approach to achieve desired results. This goes for the board of directors as well. They shouldn't be individually speaking to the media about DMO issues unless the chair has approved it, because they may mistakenly convey the impression that they are the official spokesperson for your organization when they are indeed not. (This should be thoroughly outlined in an appropriate board job description).

- **Honor the reporter's deadlines.** Editors vehemently complain when destination contacts sometimes take an extended period of time to get back to them following their requests. You will not endear your agency nor inspire confidence as a communications partner if you don't respect the media's deadline needs.

- **Avoid creating contentious relationships** with the media. For example, a reporter writes a negative piece about your agency without thoroughly checking his conclusions, and as a result, there are numerous inaccuracies. Some DMO executives on the receiving end have been so upset as to suggest that the publication issue a retraction. That, however, is ill-considered advice. When was the last time you saw a retraction of this nature? By asking for the story to be retracted, you will inflame the publication's personnel and negate a positive future relationship. Instead, ask for a meeting with the editor and the offending writer. Calmly present the facts and offer to be a constructive part of the solution going forward, providing fact checking, verification, quotes, etc.

- **Confront a negative piece quickly**. To pre-empt the spread of this harmful material, send a copy of the offending article, plus your response, to DMO board leadership and other appropriate stakeholders. Many of them may not have actually seen the negative article, but you should want them to have seen it, along with your positive response. It is through this candid, transparent approach that you will strengthen your communication's alliances. You will always need others to understand public issues from your agency's perspective and to speak up when needed on your behalf and that of the industry.

- **Produce and instill favorable impressions** for your organization over time with positive media relationships. But these efforts must be proactive, not initiated after negative coverage has occurred.

- **Cement good will and mutual respect** by meeting with editorial boards of publications at least annually. Use this as an opportunity to present positive information, backgrounders, industry trends, etc. But don't use this meeting to bring up your concerns about negative coverage. That's not the appropriate forum.

Here's a checklist of other productive communications opportunities that are available for your use as well:

- **Use letters to the editor** from you as well as your constituents. Positive responses should always be favored.

- **Proactively use the Op-Ed page,** which can work wonders. But don't use this pulpit for anything other than positive developments and vision, not negative issues or thinking.
- **Get to know the Editorial Page writers** on a personal basis. It's an important part of relationship building, just as your sales team is involved daily in the business of relationship selling.
- **Be regarded as a reliable, willing resource** for media information. This will give you the chance to speak on background and for non-attribution. There's no better way to build a stronger, more credible reputation for both you and your agency.
- **Consider establishing a regularly scheduled** monthly or quarterly community-wide round table of PR representatives to plan and enhance your communications process—one that helps everyone share information and participate in media-relations planning.
- **Don't overlook the use of association meetings** and other public forums throughout the community to effectively tell your story year round.
- **Develop a speaker's bureau** of key stakeholders or members of the board to get the right messages out consistently and quickly when the need arises.
- **Develop a crisis communications management plan** that can be quickly implemented for addressing a number of tourism challenges—from natural or manmade disasters, to energy shortfalls and economic impediments. The best advice is to do it now, because after the situation occurs is usually too late for effective implementation—and you must be prepared to quickly deal with customer perceptions and the realities of short- and long-term impacts to your industry.

The media is a powerful influence in shaping both constituent and consumer opinions for DMOs and in attracting visitor attention, awareness, and interest to visit.

The question is: how do you address this important issue in your daily communications plan for stakeholders, government officials, local residents, and others to be identified?

The answer should be through the positive positioning of your organization with the community as detailed in your annual marketing plan.

Developing the Comprehensive DMO Public Relations Plan

Your broad-based PR plan should actually be comprised of several individual plans—each one designed for and targeted to various publics.

All of them should employ a variety of PR strategies and disciplines, which are collectively integrated for optimum results. You could refer to this final plan as a rolling document in that it can be changed and added to, depending on varied situations. It should be incorporated in the organization's annual marketing plan, either in one section or segmented and placed throughout.

Positive relations fostered by these plans, over time, should result in co-operative action that will advance the DMO's core mission.

Dependent on the many communications objectives of the organization, the numerous publics and attendant plans may include the following:

1. Customer Plan—Supports management's objective of developing and retaining business from each market segment. Generally speaking, the PR function supports the marketing requirement of producing awareness and resulting interest in both the DMO and the destination it represents. Market segments include, among others,

- meetings and conventions: planners, association CEOs, association members
- group tours: tour operators, tour brokers, and their potential customers
- leisure discretionary consumers
- independent business travelers
- consumer and trade media
- national media (for brand development): this may be a stand-alone plan or a support component for the customer plan.

2. Community Relations/Public Affairs Plan—Creates and enhances a positive and favorable environment in which the DMO can fulfill its mission. Publics include

- the local general public
- government agencies and their employees
- local media, including editorial board, business and travel writers, etc. (This is sometimes placed under a publicity or media relations category.)

3. Stakeholder Relations Plan—Produces business partnerships, alliances, and ultimately additional revenue and marketing resources for DMO marketing. Publics include

- members/partners
- related economic development, cultural and tourism related agencies, organizations, and businesses
- key constituent groups, the convention center, hotels, senior government partners.

4. Crisis Management Plan—Assuages public and media concerns that exacerbate the actual negative situation, providing comprehensive, timely, factual information. Examples include major crime and public disturbances, acts of terrorism, and gasoline embargoes. This component includes both prevention and execution.

5. Internal Relations Plan—Assures a healthy, positive, productive workplace for all employees. Human relations/administration usually administers this function.

Bill Gates has been quoted as saying, "If I was down to my last dollar, I'd spend it on public relations."

By implementing this comprehensive DMO PR program, you'll greatly enhance your reputation and favorability with customers that Mr. Gates—and many others—are surely likely to appreciate and applaud.

How To Field the Really Tough Questions with the Absolutely Correct Answers

It's time to get on your toes for this three-question pop quiz that addresses how to handle constituent (and sometimes adversarial) questions with responses that are sure to build positive points for you in the stakeholder/ community relations arena.

SCENARIO/QUESTION 1: This morning you find yourself on the agenda for the city council meeting. It's going to be your job to convince everyone of the value of your DMO's positive work on behalf of the community. They have a really packed agenda, so you'll have little more than ten or fifteen minutes to make a positive impression. What do you decide to say?

ANSWER 1: First, forget about the ten to fifteen minutes. Yes, I know you've been given the allotted time, but your message will be much more memorable if it's on target and you keep it brief; then if questions are asked, you've still got plenty of time to respond.

Don't start by telling them about the size and scope of the tourism industry there, how important it is in producing jobs, and the millions in visitor receipts and tax revenues expended by travelers. If you do that first, it will sound like you and your organization are solely responsible for this success story—and you've just taken the opportunity to publicly pat yourself on the back.

Instead, begin by sharing with them your DMO mission statement. And then specifically tell them what your organization actually delivered in response to it last year, with the strong value statement that I hope you've created by adding up all your quantifiable productivity results from sales, direct marketing, and media publicity. Your strong ROI should impress everyone.

You may also share your board's vision for your organization and how you plan to chart a long-term course for success on behalf of all constituents, including government, through your positive public-private community partnership.

A Value Statement Case Study

This value statement approach was initially developed for a major CVB that was on the verge of losing major funding from one of its government partners. The CEO had consistently tried to tell the story to these government officials, but their focus was always about trying to explain how important the tourism industry was in total expenditures or what the CVB had delivered in marketing activity: sales, trade shows, collateral material, media attention, publications, website visits, and advertising.

But none of this was persuading the mayor not to cut the CVB's budget allocation. In fact, he told the CEO that he was going to take the money and use it for police protection, beach replenishment, and some local advertising.

Then, as a last resort, the DMO altered its approach at our direction. For their next meeting with the city council and the mayor, the CEO concentrated solely on what they had quantifiably accomplished for the city through their newly developed value statement: visitors and visitor dollars produced through advertising and website development programs, conventions booked, and delegate expenditures delivered to the community, along with positive media publicity valued in the millions that influenced favorable opinion and consumer intent to visit.

The city's positive response to their report was immediate. They unanimously approved an extension to the CVB contract and full funding for the next five years.

SCENARIO/QUESTION 2: Recognizing that tourism is such big business for your community, and that your CVB is responsible for helping to grow it, how do you quantify the size and scope of it all?

ANSWER 2: This won't be difficult to provide—if you have an annual economic impact study that measures total visitor receipts, tax revenue produced, businesses serving travelers, and local jobs generated or sustained through visitor spending. There are a number of reliable sources for producing this report through econometric modeling, and you certainly need this data to monitor the industry's growth and to share its ongoing value with your constituents.

Armed with this economic data, you can probably answer other important questions such as the following:

- How is our destination doing in relationship to others? In other words, what's your market share over time compared to the state's growth rate and that of nearby regional competitors? If you're low, there's a message to give about the need for additional DMO market funding. If you're high, then you may be on solid footing but will always need to strengthen your program funding to stay competitive. But having and sharing the economic story for your community is just the first step.

- Who is your visitor? Particularly the profile of your leisure visitors; where they reside, what motivates them to visit, what are their demographic characteristics (geographic point of origination, age, income, educational level, etc.) as well as their psychographic profile (their likes, desires, attitudes, interests, etc.).

Can you envision how your local partners could readily profit from this visitor market study and profile, including what visitors know and don't know about your destination, specifically what motivates their interest, and what would bring them back again and again? A new attraction, new events, diverse shopping experiences, or other amenities?

It's surprising that so few have this valuable market data, because it's certainly available from several industry research companies; can you imagine a corporate market research firm not having this information?

SCENARIO/QUESTION 3: How is your organization doing in the fulfillment of its mission that works to produce incremental business for my local business, property, attraction, or service?

This question goes to the heart of your constituent relationships. It seeks to determine how well stakeholders understand and truly value the work you do, the mission you fulfill, and the collaborative results you achieve.

Can you answer with great reliability how pleased your hoteliers are with your efforts?

Or how, in comparison, do other major industry segments view your work, including attractions, events, restaurants, retail, the arts community, transportation companies—even local elected officials.

The same question can be posed to your customers: how do meeting planners and tour operators, for example, perceive your destination product and the service it delivers for them?

ANSWER 3: The only reliably objective method for answering this question is by implementing stakeholder/customer assessment surveys that provide an effective barometer for how your DMO's work is perceived.

More DMOs are initiating this approach. While some handle the surveys in-house, the third-party independent survey approach allows partners and clients to speak freely and provide the most candid appraisals.

Just remember: you can't correct what is not acknowledged. Once you have this assessment information, and can learn any specific concerns expressed by individuals and various business segments, you can work with your staff to develop positive responses to address and ameliorate their concerns, both perceptual and real.

Is Your Organization
the Community's Chief Cheerleader?

Producing quantifiable business results is certainly a major component of your operational mission. But another—and often undervalued and misunderstood requirement—is its role in building community goodwill, understanding, and support for the organization's work, while serving as a community leader.

Early in my career, when preparing to become president of the Memphis CVB, I had a career-changing experience at a welcoming cocktail party.

The soiree at a posh home overlooking the mighty Mississippi was attended by many of the city's top community, business, and government leadership. Niceties and "good lucks" were offered throughout the evening. And then I found myself sitting next to a pleasant, distinguished-looking, white-haired gentleman whom everyone seemed to know and admire. His name was John Burton Tigrett.

I later discovered that he had been the financial consultant for world-renowned business tycoon Armand Hammer, noted in his own right as one of America's most innovative entrepreneurs and deal makers, and unquestionably one of the most perceptive and influential people I've ever met. It was Tigrett who had been asked to shepherd the economic development funding partnership plan between local government and its corporate leaders, including Federal Express, First Tennessee Bank, and the Holiday Corporation that had brought me to Memphis to develop an expanded, revitalized convention and visitors bureau.

"So tell me about your plans," John Tigrett asked with an engaging smile.

I was midway through a prepared list of tactics—triple the staff; launch a new ad campaign; establish sales offices in DC, Chicago, and New York—when he politely halted me in mid-stream.

"Thanks for that," he said graciously. Then he leaned forward in a posture of confidentiality, placed his hand on my shoulder as you would with a young son and quietly began, "Now let me tell you what's really going on here and what your role should be in it.

"It wasn't so long ago that Dr. Martin Luther King was assassinated here," he explained, "and a lot of our town folk are still reeling from that, feeling responsible, embarrassed, and so on. . . . And as you've no doubt already discovered, there's also a general malaise throughout our hospitality industry, with no clear direction.

"Let me put it to you another way," Tigrett said slowly with hushed emphasis.

"In case you haven't noticed, there's a wild elephant running loose in this town. And your job, my friend, is to get on top of that animal, grab it firmly by the ears, and turn it around."

Tigrett spoke with conviction as he described the CVB's new role as he saw and felt it. "And then with a growing parade of bureau stakeholders, government and industry leaders, and the public behind you, and with bands playing and flag's flying, you and your board need to steer that elephant in the right path forward, heading through town, with everyone cheering and participating in this exciting new program for Memphis's future."

As Tigrett finished his drink, he looked me squarely in the eye, smiled again warmly, and said, "And that, young man, is your number-one assignment and challenge. So the best of luck to you." He smiled and offered a handshake, "and please do count me as your friend in this endeavor."

That meeting and its message hit me square between the eyes. And it forever changed my whole perspective about the task at hand and my plans for the Memphis CVB.

I set aside my business-oriented proposed marketing plan for a while and began to concentrate on John Tigrett's directional charge and challenge: to chart an exciting new program of community understanding, involvement, and participation.

Our board of directors enthusiastically concurred. With our new program, the bureau needed to become, and be clearly recognized as, the community leader for economic development through tourism. We had to rally community pride in Memphis, serve as the community's chief tourism cheerleading organization, and lead the charge for hospitality industry partnership support, necessary infrastructural changes, service excellence, and long-range visioning. That wild elephant running through town just had to go.

Some of the numerous tactics included in the Memphis program were

- a public launch of "Start Something Great in Memphis," the new public service campaign featuring ongoing public service TV, radio, and print coverage that garnered strong public support
- the Memphis Tourism Summit provided a roll-out of the bureau's new marketing plan to three hundred local tourism stakeholders, along with key invited national business leaders who came and later touted the program that garnered rave reviews from the nation's leisure travel and meetings industry sectors; every top national leader association sent their CEO to see what all the fuss was about, including the Travel Industry Association of America, the Society of American Travel Writers, the American Society of Association Executives, the National Tourism Association, American Bus, and American Society of Travel Agents
- Memphis front-line travel employees signed up for the new citywide educational training program

- a speaker's bureau of CVB volunteers took the "Tourism Works for Memphis" story to numerous civic associations
- both the city and the county mayors headed up the CVB's new Memphis Road Show to New York, DC, and Chicago to call on customers, travel writers, tour operators, and meeting planners for the first time
- local media coverage consistently touted the success of the Memphis bureau and its members
- the Travel Industry Association of America recognized Memphis with a top national award for marketing excellence.

The biggest surprise occurred two and a half years after the "Start Something Great" campaign launch, when estimated community tourism expenditures for that period grew from $600,000 annually to more than $1 billion, according to the US Travel Data Center. Was any of this attributable to the campaign? Though no such claims were made, many leaders believed there was a compelling, catalytic effect.

Today's successful DMO must concentrate on three success factors:

- performance of economic development benefits in fulfilling its core mission
- marketing and management excellence through its research, planning, execution, and evaluative steps
- being the recognized leader in the community for tourism development—well regarded for its local visible leadership position with stakeholders, while fulfilling a leadership role for infrastructure requirements, visitor amenities, and service issues.

Other Recommendations

I have found that the key to developing and valuing this public initiative for leadership is to clearly annunciate and then list this objective:

*To provide community leadership that flows from
the DMO's mission statement*

For some DMOs and their CEOs, this program is an integral part of their day-to-day mission.

Today, Memphis CVB President Kevin Kane and Greater Miami CVB's Bill Talbert both handle this assignment as if they'd been born to it. That's because each of them is truly involved throughout their communities and live their positions through leadership that doesn't end after the office closes its doors.

Delivering this kind of DMO-focused community leadership requires a commitment to participate and communicate with other community organizations on an ongoing basis and to work with the Chamber of Commerce, downtown development groups, arts council, elected and appointed officials, and so many other constituent organizations. The most successful DMOs also encourage their staff management to join these associations and share their interests and expertise as committee members or officers.

Other organizational leadership initiatives include long-range visioning, strategic planning, and public advocacy.

Never underestimate the power of community constituents in helping to bring about a stronger and more cohesive DMO effort for your destination.

How To Hire, Fire, and Manage

Sooner or later, you'll likely be asked to supervise or hire others. If you're not prepared, there aren't crash courses available in real-world management. You won't find many of these recommendations in textbooks or available from most human resource officers, nor are today's managers universally applying these techniques. If they were, employees would be far more successful and fulfilled and organizations would be more stable and productive.

How to Hire

It should be a given that you only hire people who clearly possess the necessary skills to fulfill the position. The optimum approach should be for you to always hire the best people for the position at hand (subject to required salary ranges provided).

But how do you most effectively assess their core competencies and past performance and accomplishments to determine if they're best equipped for your team?

- **Recognize that it's a waste of time trying to evaluate potential hires based on the references that they provide.** Most of those accolades will be from friends who will hardly be objective. Nor can you rely on the candidate's former employers to share reliable input—because to avoid potential future litigation from employees who may have been dismissed or who left under unfavorable circumstances, personnel departments are unlikely to provide you with anything more than confirmation of their previous employment and dates of service.

- **Focus on querying others in their field of work that may be their peer competitors**—both within and outside the organizations for whom they've worked. Probe their professional opinions about the person you're considering.

- **Check out the candidate's volunteer and public service record.** Few do this, but it'll be an excellent indicator of their personal drive, passion, and social commitment.

- **Don't hire political cronies.** Sometime during your career, you're going to be asked, as a favor, to hire someone connected or political. This could be a friend of the boss, a stakeholder, or someone simply who is owed a personal favor by others in high places. Do everything you can to avoid this no-win situation. Because if they're incompetent—and many will surely be—you're screwed three times: first, they won't be capable of accomplishing your mission; second, other competent employees will resent their presence, the inequity of paying them for nonperformance, and, most of all, you for employing them in the first place; and third, you won't be able to easily extricate them from the office.

I succumbed to this situation only once, and it turned out to be a maddening experience. The employee wasn't nearly as qualified as I had surmised. To make matters worse, the individual wasn't trained to adequately supervise others either. Things quickly got worse when the department transposed the telephone number of our visitor call center with that of an evening gentlemen's club. The error wasn't discovered by the supervisor until tens of thousands of new tourism brochures bearing the strip club's phone number had been printed and distributed—and then we had no choice but to go behind the scenes to pay thousands of dollars to buy that club's phone number and take it out of circulation.

If you absolutely have no way out and are forced by management to hire a political crony, try to buffer your daily emotional well-being by positioning them between a manager and you.

- **Have a game plan established for this position**—not just a general job description, but also a review of how you envision this person playing a key role on your team. Remember, every single employee is special. Demonstrate that fact in the hiring process.

Provide a list of personal, ongoing performance objectives: not what the individual will do, but what they will specifically achieve—in other words, how they will help the team to score points and win games. Include the percentage of time you anticipate each personal performance objective to take and their specific role in an ongoing collaborative team effort of integration.

- **Seek out self-motivated people to join your team.** Motivating others is a difficult task. Consider all the ways people try to motivate others and still fail miserably: We promise stiff penalties for crimes against society, but our prison systems keep building more cells to incarcerate the guilty. And while we try rehabilitation to motivate positive behavior, the rate of recidivism hasn't dramatically improved in many quarters. We provide positive feedback to employees; deliver incentive compensation, training, employee-assistance programs, and other benefits. Yet job retention throughout corporate America of skilled workers is still a major employment issue—and that's expensive in retraining and retooling.

Just look around you at the people who aren't as happy and apparently as socially adjusted as most others. You can usually see it in their demeanor, carriage, and eyes. They're the pessimistic ones who appear to be most dissatisfied with not only their work, but also their lot in life—and it's displayed consistently in how they interact with others, their personal relationships, their perception of society and government, what they think they are owed, etc. I submit they also lack motivation.

These are the very people whom you must identify and then avoid during the candidate-seeking process. Instead, be on the lookout for only those who are self-motivated. They'll be best suited to be a part of a winning, productive team where almost anything can become possible.

- **Evaluate and test candidates.** Learn more about the use of behavioral interviewing with questions that are designed to test the true technical abilities and actual achievements of your candidates. Apply team interviewing with your staff whenever feasible, and develop scorecards for use that are built around ideal candidate profiles. You should always evaluate by pretesting candidates—or at least the top three for any given position—through a third-party process. One proven method is to use a series of what-if case scenarios to assess their abilities to make reasoned judgments.

How to Fire

No, you obviously can't and wouldn't even think about emulating Donald Trump's "You're fired" *Apprentice* TV approach. (Well, maybe you would think about it, depending on how badly you wanted to terminate a poorly performing employee who's wreaking havoc in the office.) Here's how to effectively deal with employee terminations.

- **Make a habit of removing unproductive, unhappy people.** Most employees who are capable of good work but just aren't fulfilling their responsibilities are, in many cases, unmotivated, unhappy individuals. These people are toxic. And you need to focus on eliminating them from your organization by whatever means feasible. Early in my career, I knew a national executive with the millions of membered AAA Motor Club, who had inherited a senior manager with severe morale and performance liabilities. He tried a half-dozen approaches to encourage and motivate this person, but finally realized that like so many cases of this nature, this person just simply wasn't very joyous about anything—certainly not his job. And so that's what the executive focused on—the person's unhappiness.

"You just don't seem to want to be here, doing what is required in this position—and I sympathize with you. It's just not the right fit for you, is it?" The recalcitrant employee reluctantly agreed and left the company. That's just the type of discussion you need to have with unmotivated, unhappy employees who are adversely affecting the morale and performance of your team.

Sometimes, during their transition out, you'll need to help them with financial assistance or extended benefits. Don't hesitate to consider providing these conciliatory offers because in the long run they will be well worth the price and costs versus the alternative. Just be sure you apply this approach with ongoing fairness and equity to other employee situations.

- **Take unproductive employees through steps of progressive discipline.** When there's no possibility of separation of service based on the first scenario, you must provide ongoing personal monitoring and feedback to the employee about what they are doing that's unacceptable and why—specifically, how they are not fulfilling their personal performance objectives or the terms of their performance contract (a recommendation I make in the next section of this chapter).

If you don't do this, and instead give them okay annual evaluations, you won't have documentation of their failings—and you will be on shaky ground when you later decide to take corrective action.

Progressive discipline requires you to (1) consistently document your notes about employee's poor performance, (2) personally review these issues with the employee, and (3) offer coaching and support when they request it. Progressively, these warnings should escalate from verbal to written, with attendant penalties that can eventually lead to dismissal. (And here again, you may eventually need to revisit point one above about removing unproductive, unhappy people.)

Following the verbal and written warnings, employees should be given a performance improvement plan, with explicit action plans containing timelines and regular meetings to review progress in relation to the plans. These meetings all require documentation. There also needs to be a time limit on the plan (60–90 days) with a clear understanding that failure to meet the requirements of the action plan will result in termination. And if the employee is failing, you need to follow through and terminate; your failure to do so is an extremely negative message to the organization.

A cautionary note: Be sure you don't take any of these steps without first seeking guidance from legal counsel and HR. Then work as a team to prevent future employee relations complications.

How to Manage

I warned earlier that you can't be expected to motivate employees. But what you must do is provide a constructive environment that allows for an individual's self-motivation. This includes the following ten strategies:

- **The 360-degree review.** This review involves the confidential evaluation of managers by their peers and immediate subordinates. We recommend its usage to help strengthen the organization and the relationships of the staff.

- **No surprises.** Above all, this means creating a workplace of transparency, understanding, candor, and openness, where there are no surprises for anyone.

- **Full disclosure.** Everyone should know the ground rules about all issues, with the exception of proprietary competitive information. A well-designed, up-to-date personnel policy and procedures manual that all employees have is a must. And they should be required to sign and thus acknowledge its contents.

- **An ethics policy.** The policy should be publicly posted and signed by all. It should state what is unacceptable and won't be tolerated; from nepotism to favoritism, to violations of honesty, trust, and respect for individuals. The policy shouldn't be written by management, but instead by the rank-and-file employees who comprise the core of the organization. Use an outside professional facilitator for assistance and direction. Or start with a standard policy, then discuss and approve each section.

- **Performance pledge.** An employee personnel manual should never be designed as an implied contract with an employee that guarantees employment come rain or shine. Nor am I suggesting a written document that binds the employer in perpetuity to the employee. However,

I favor the use of an individual pledge or written and signed commitment between the employee and employer that asks for the staffer's best ongoing efforts in fulfilling the personal performance objectives. And the employee should agree to abide by both the personnel policy standards and its ethics policy.

- **Office operations committee.** Comprise a self-chosen representative handful of rank-and-file employees who meet regularly to discuss and advise management on employee concerns and questions.

- **Four P meetings.** The most effective process for avoiding surprises is through ongoing, regularly scheduled, productive, but brief, four P meetings (Plans, Progress, Problems, and Plans—a process developed by Wil Brewer of Performance Solutions). They should be held weekly. Each meeting should be no more than ten to fifteen minutes and require employees to complete the four Ps in advance of the meeting with their managers.

So whether you're managing up or managing down, here is how you should structure these meetings, prepared in writing, on a single sheet of paper:

- **Begin with Plans,** prioritizing and summarizing the agreed-upon plans or assignments that you're now undertaking or that your staff is initiating as previously confirmed with you.
- **Review the Progress of project completion**, detailing the step-by-step work to date, concluding with anticipated timeline completion dates as they conform to the agreed-upon schedule.
- **Outline any Problems you are facing** in carrying out your assignment. (Here's where most fail, in being willing to candidly assess and report concerns, challenges, or impediments to management.) You must be willing to fairly appraise this situation. And it's also important to be prepared to offer suggested solutions. But you can also ask for collaborative advice, assistance, and management support at this time. New, agreed-upon timelines may then be established.
- **End with Plans.** These may remain the same or change as appropriate to meet changing circumstances or requirements.

- **Establishing deadlines.** This may come as a surprise to you, but as a manager, you should avoid setting project deadlines for employee assignments except in rare cases when there are unusual time constraints imposed by you or your senior management. Instead, you should require staff assigned to the task to set and adhere to their own deadlines, which you should merely approve and monitor as part of ongoing four P reports. After all, they are best equipped to know how much time it will take to best fit the operational requirements for this work into their own delivery of additional commitments. To supersede their judgment in forecasting timelines, over time, will minimize their responsibility, authority, and morale.

- **Fulfilling deadlines.** Timelines established by the staff are meant to be kept. It's a commitment to everyone on the team. Moreover, if deadlines are anticipated to be missed, employees are responsible for giving everyone advance notice that there will be a delay—along with providing a new firm future date for project completion.

- **Policies, procedures, implementation outlines.** A company can be measured by the how-to-do-it documents it keeps and follows. All programs and policies, like the four P meetings and the deadlines established, should be memorialized in writing for the entire staff. Remember, no surprises. Program implementation outlines should include

  - program objective
  - steps to completion
  - manpower and financial resources required
  - methods for evaluating program success
  - names/positions of those who must sign off on the process.

Are You the Problem?

Finally, pay attention to how you behave and whether negative situations in your office are due to your previous inattention to personnel needs. Perhaps you just might be part of the problem.

Ask your employees how you're doing or what they suggest could be done differently.

It's a serious fact that employees can be demotivated and may be performing poorly as a result of bad management—a bad boss. An estimated 61 percent of employees leave their jobs on account of their managers. So look inward; you just might be an important part of the future solution as well.

Employee Performance:
Best Pay for Performance Practices

Your greatest asset is your staff. And compensating employees fairly and equitably is the first step in showing your organization's appreciation for the significant contributions they achieve.

Incentive-based compensation for employees is a best practice for maximizing performance. Instead of straight salary or occasional bonus programs, the incentive part of compensation is recognized as a component of salary that is set aside at the beginning of each year and awarded quarterly for achieving or exceeding predetermined goals.

The payout amounts are based on percentages of annual compensation, ranging from perhaps 10–25 percent of annual salary for direct sales personnel to 5–15 percent for other marketing deliverables such as media publicity and membership development. Team incentives can also be incorporated and have shown to be important in boosting morale, team spirit, employee initiative, and performance results.

Implement incentive plans whenever they are feasible and will fit the organization's culture and business model. In other cases, I suggest a modification of incentive compensation for employees that is still tied to both quantitative and qualitative achievement criteria.

How To Compensate Based on a Modified Incentive Plan

The first step in the process is developing employee criteria for evaluation. This requires a disciplined, written business model that incorporates as much objective criteria as possible, including both qualitative and quantitative components whenever feasible.

First, let's focus on the CEO. Then later, this approach can serve as a model for staff application.

Recommended evaluative criteria for the CEO's position should be reviewed and agreed to by the executive committee and CEO at the beginning of the evaluation period, usually each year. Following each year, the executive committee or compensation committee should review the executive's performance results and meet with them to provide this annual evaluation and resulting approved compensation.

Here are the standard categories included for a traditional CEO evaluation:

- **Qualitative components** (usually amounting to 50 percent of the evaluation). Each of these categories should be assigned a percentage, which may vary somewhat dependent on board interests, but will aggregately total 50 percent of the evaluation. If this plan is approved, it should be modified for use throughout the organization. The qualitative components include

  - board relations
  - fiscal management including budget development
  - annual marketing/business plan development and tactical execution
  - staff management
  - government and stakeholder relations
  - community leadership.

- **Quantitative components** (usually amounting to 50 percent of the evaluation). These should be based on predetermined goals established by the CEO and agreed to by the board at the beginning of the evaluation period. Again, these categories may be weighted, with some receiving a higher percentage, but in the aggregate totaling 50 percent of the entire evaluation. The quantitative components include

  - booked convention business
  - group tour bookings
  - visitor conversion and economic impacts through advertising/website
  - media publicity produced
  - sports programs produced, film development, etc.
  - other criteria as agreed to by the CEO and board or executive committee.

All of these written criteria should be spelled out in detail as part of an enhanced job description for the CEO. The board may also include additional personal performance objectives or deliverables with the advance understanding of the CEO.

Put these compensation processes to work, and you'll be pleased to see employee performance increase over time, because this is a best practice for tying pay to performance and rewarding employees appropriately for the accomplishments they deliver.

Business Ethics and the Ego of Conceit

Here are some views you're not likely to hear from others about the root cause of our ethics dilemma in today's business environment.

Throughout my consultancy career, I've been fortunate to work with some great DMO executives and their staffs in helping to develop strategic planning assignments and the positive results they've achieved.

But unfortunately, you probably know me best as the auditing consultant for many communities that were having operational challenges and needed outside guidance—at least that was the opinion of their DMO boards, their government officials, or other senior community leadership constituents.

Although that auditing work doesn't make up more than 10 percent of my ongoing business, it certainly accounted for 90 percent of the media attention that I infamously attracted—and it surely stamped me with a reputation of someone to be avoided.

Just before I was hired for an international auditing assignment, the CVB chairman told me an unnamed reference had described me this way: "If you have something to hide, don't hire Murdaugh, because he'll find it." Truth be told, that's what mostly has happened. I've uncovered some interesting scenarios:

- In one major West Coast CVB, they reported the cancellation of forty-four major booked conventions over a three-year period. That issue raised a lot of concerns in the hotel community, convention center, and city government—a truly alarming and unprecedented number of cancellations, with tens of millions of dollars in unrealized delegate spending and unfilled room nights. Through our analysis, we soon discovered that these conventions had never actually attained the status of confirmed bookings—so they never became canceled business—yet over a three-year period, the CVB sales staff who worked these accounts, as well as senior management who oversaw them, received hefty and undeserved incentive compensation for business that was never initially booked. Some would call this fraud.

- In another nearby community, the finance director stole more than $50,000 in operational funds under the nose of the DMO executive director. Then we determined that prior to the theft, fiscal management systems were deficient, despite written and verbal warnings and management letters issued earlier by the CPA to the CEO that were never heeded. Some would call this financial management malfeasance.

- On the East Coast, a mid-sized CVB was found to have padded its performance results for bookings and quantifiable results with seriously flawed numbers, even going so far as to use the CEO's Christmas card mailing list to expand the organization's membership roles—and then he and another staffer who oversaw these indiscretions received incentive compensation at year's end.

Things Are Improving

Fortunately, these flagrant examples make up a very small segment of DMO performance liability concerns. Nor are many audits centered on the issue of performance productivity. Performance today is less of an issue because most DMOs are taking performance management seriously, supported by the needs of their business and government constituents and the solid leadership work of the Destination Marketing Association International in developing industry business performance standards, ongoing educational programs, and new professional certification programs for senior executives and the DMO as an organization.

Perhaps it is because of this positive situation that the need for performance management and marketing audits appears to be diminishing, and that's a promising sign.

Key Audit Recommendations

Whenever I've concluded a performance management audit, my recommendations have always been highlighted by

- the need for legal and ethical standards through a comprehensive policy of ethics for staff and board including conflicts of business interests; acceptance of gifts; a personal and financial code of conduct; and other requirements for integrity, transparency, honesty, and accountability
- implementation of industry standard management procedures and policies
- establishment of industry best business practices for performance marketing
- professional industry association membership and accreditation of the organization and staff
- third-party expert validation of performance results.

These recommendations have had a positive impact in helping many DMOs become more performance driven and successful.

Today's Big Challenge

Yet even with these recommendations and precautions, there are still roadblocks and impediments that adversely challenge today's business environment—and not just with DMOs. That ongoing fundamental challenge is what I call the ego of conceit.

What is *ego*? It is defined as the psychic apparatus or the part of us that experiences and reacts to the outside world. It's the *I* or *self* of anyone, as thinking, feeling, and willing, that distinguishes ourselves from others.

However, that is not the ego of conceit. My focus is on egotism, or ego-centric behavior, as it destructively impedes the good work of organizations and individuals. Too often, I've seen it manifested in arrogance, self-importance, and the expression of entitlement, of pride, of being exalted or above reproach. This egotism undermines leadership through all of its requirements that are related to governance, management, and marketing issues, as well as relationships with others—particularly with major stakeholders. It can also appear as an attitude of condescension, a patronizing behavior and an apparent disregard for the opinions of others.

When these characteristics are found in senior management of an organization, such as a DMO, it can permeate and adversely affect every component of that organization. It clouds focus and judgment, leadership and business decision making. For example:

- When there is a strong community perception of the DMO as an independent, autonomous, private organization that reports solely to its board and its members, that is an indicator of this ego-driven behavior because DMOs actually function as part of a community's public-private partnership with government, business, and the community residents it supports. It is not an island unto itself.

- When the DMO board of directors is described by constituents as a "rubber stamp" board, or as not being fully engaged, energized, or proactive, that, too, is the fundamental fault of executive management's egotism in controlling the organization for their own purposes. Instead, the president should have provided the board with an adequate job description, a board code of conduct, bylaw recommendations, and guidelines for producing standard board policy and action—all the requirements for an active board that can best support the DMO.

- When stakeholders overwhelmingly express concern about the development of marketing programs and staff management that never sought their input or collaboration, that too is a sign of management's ego of conceit.

- When the DMO has an ethics policy in place that calls for avoidance of conflicts of interest, yet there are vendors who sit on the board of directors who, through their positions, have responsibility for management oversight of the CEO at the same time they financially profit from their vendor relationship in doing business with the organization; yes, that is certainly another sign of special, inappropriate privilege and egotism at work.

- When the CEO's leadership role is driven by ego and is, therefore, not open to ideas, suggestions, or creative thinking from staff, executives, the board, or stakeholders, this is particularly negative for the organization, because it minimizes the willingness of other executives and rank-and-file staff to challenge ideas and to enable the CEO to confront the brutal facts and situations swirling around them.

Remedies for Egotism

Termination is an obvious response. Coaching may also have merit, starting with 360-degree reviews and behavioral intelligence assessments. In general, it also calls for the board to step up and demand increased levels of accountability for all aspects of the operation—yet that is sometimes a difficult task for a volunteer board.

But the long-term approach in addressing this dysfunctional challenge is to be mindful of egotism at all levels and how it can consistently interfere in how we live our lives and the way we approach our work in making decisions and interfacing with others.

It's easy to understand why some experts describe ego as our silent partner—too often with a controlling interest. According to Deepak Chopra, an authority on mind-body healing, the key to success is to consistently try to go beyond your ego. "Make a decision to relinquish the need to control, the need to be approved, and the need to judge," he urged. "Those are the three things the ego is doing all the time. It's very important to be aware of them every time they come up."

One suggested guidepost for keeping egos in check can be the vision statement (see chapter 1), which contains the many qualities we should work to emulate. However, successfully modeling its many required attributes and qualities—including candor, transparency, fairness, and other principles—is solely dependent on how well we follow the approach with honesty and integrity.

CHAPTER 5
Flash Points

"It is not the strongest of the species that survive, not the most intelligent, but the one most responsive to change."
—Charles Darwin

How to Increase Destination Market Share

In the midst of any serious economic malaise, there's actually a silver lining for DMOs: the opportunity to grow destination market share.

Turbulent economic downturns for the consumer have always spelled exceedingly tough times for the travel industry . . . attendant job losses . . . travelers curtailing trips or staying closer to home and spending less . . . while triggering other resultant losses in the spending cycle. The negative effects can be substantial and continuous.

But periods of economic downturn are also a time to strengthen and solidify your program by focusing on this extremely important marketing axiom:

It is during economic downturns that DMOs have the very best opportunity for increasing destination market share.

That is because market share doesn't shift during good times when the total economic pie traditionally grows and most destinations get their share and can prosper. Instead, it can best increase during times of economic downturn—with lower average daily rate, less hotel room nights sold, and reductions in the bed tax and destination marketing budgets.

That situation creates a dynamic when some DMOs may pull back and when some savvy competitors can catch a new paradigm by increasing either their budget or their programming that will produce an increased share of voice and customer awareness and resulting market share in relationship to the competition.

No one ever said this is an easy task. Yet some strategic thinking DMOs have always been able to make this occur at the expense of others. It requires proactive thinking and taking advantage of a deteriorating economy to develop new collaborative programs with stakeholders, to partner with their communities to increase their share of hotel transient taxes to reinvest back into marketing programming, and to revisit their marketing plans to seek innovative ways to increase staff activity and attendant performance results.

There's no better time to address tourism's benefits to your community because it is through tourism that we can quickly provide a positive engine of economic development and economic recovery, without having to go out and build new businesses to create jobs.

Sometimes we aren't mindful that the value of tourism is a truly powerful story to tell, and this is the very best time to share it with everyone.

The Funding Development Plan for Destination Success

At the very top of the list of ongoing DMO needs is the requirement for additional funding that opens new doors for economic recovery and visitor expansion. Therefore, it should be the centerpiece of your action plan.

In our experience, some of the most effective organizational funding action plans have garnered truly great success, producing funding increases in the 40–300 percent annual range. And while we all recognize that DMOs and destination challenges are never the same, here are some of the most important issues and resulting tactics that have brought about this success in the CVB community.

The good news is that they have actually occurred in both good economic times as well as during economic downturns.

We have focused on the transient occupancy tax (TOT) as the principal funding source, but these key program requirements may also be applied to other funding requirements, including voluntary assessments and BID programs.

1. Protect Your Existing Funding

Before we get started on the action plan, let's address the ongoing threat to the traditional number-one resource for CVBs, the dedicated TOT that fuels nearly 90 percent of today's bureaus. And make no mistake; it's your role to proactively protect it. That's because today, only about 55 percent of the local TOT on average is being earmarked for CVBs.

Unfortunately, a lot of this money goes to non-tourist-related local uses, which is challenging as well as dangerously counterproductive, according to a national study from the Hotel & Lodging Educational Foundation. This study, which is periodically updated, concludes that increases in the hotel tax, for non-CVB marketing (city general fund, arts council operating expenses, heritage preservation, beach and waterfront development, sports facilities, arenas, etc.), can actually cause reductions in local tourism business through the reduced room sales and associated visitor spending that then negatively affects every sector of the local economy—a 2 percent increase in national taxes on visitors, for example, would reduce an estimated 300,000 jobs and billions of dollars in unrealized visitor spending.

Our recommendation is to become thoroughly familiar with this study and then disseminate it as required to protect the integrity of this important marketing resource for your organization and the community you serve.

2. Support Your New Funding Need through Research

Your first action plan step is developing a persuasive argument for new funding through research. The checklist includes the following actions:

- Compare your budget to other successful competitors, and show your annual diminished budget if the annual growth rates and percentage of TOT allocation are higher.
- If your organization is less than the size of the average DMO in both funding and staffing, state that as well. (The DMAI Annual Organizational and Financial Profile is an important resource to use.)
- Compare your community to other more successful destinations based on a wide range of competitive sets (convention center size, rooms within proximity, airport facilities, major attractions that draw visitors, event programs, etc.).
- Use your lost business reports from the convention market to clarify to whom you are consistently losing business; then document what they're doing successfully and why you're unable to effectively respond.
- Determine your lost visitor market share from state and national data.
- Use a local travel barometer of major travel indicators (air arrivals, interstate traffic, restaurant receipts, visitor center volumes, attractions attendance, etc.) to show business trends versus state and national indicators.
- Also, don't shy away from communicating marketing challenges and weaknesses in your ongoing communications to stakeholders and business partners; if you consistently display an "Everything is Rosie" posture of false optimism for the community and DMO, few constituents will then believe in the credibility of your new concerns about the needs for additional funding.

3. Make Sure You Have Strong Community Support

Before you launch your funding action plan, make sure you have the strong support of community stakeholders as well as the local votes by the governing body.

I've worked with a variety of communities who had limited confidence in the governing board of the DMO. Others, such as the hotel, arts, and sports communities, felt they weren't appropriately represented at the board and executive committee level. The same has been found true by government officials who felt distanced by the organization and not linked with them through representation of their city manager or mayor's office. In each case, positive steps were required to ameliorate these issues first to assure good governance representation and deliver a strong message of DMO/community support and communications.

I've also discovered that while the community generally supports the DMO, they may sometimes lack confidence in its abilities to actually produce incremental business. You must initially determine the level of confidence in your organization before moving forward with a coordinated plan. Assessment techniques may include:

- **a projectable stakeholder assessment survey** that answers this question in detail: how is the DMO doing in the fulfillment of its mission statement that supports my business?
- **a validation process based** on local meetings with principal stakeholders including hoteliers and all other segments of the industry. Meetings with the local governing body or their leadership should be taken. This can be done by staff, the board members, or an independent third-party consultant. Focus groups can also be employed.

Next, be sure to do the following:

- **Create the value statement** for your DMO that states, in one succinct paragraph, what it produces in annual return on dollar investment from marketing programs on an ongoing basis—and back that up with reliable documentation.
- **Help constituents recognize that only your DMO** provides the most effective consolidated marketing model that can produce higher volumes of business for the entire community. Introduce them to the culture of the industry that you represent, with copies of the DMAI book *Fundamentals of Destination Management and Marketing*.

4. Plan and Introduce a New Marketing Program

The most effective funding program involves introducing a new marketing program or a new spin on past efforts—not just merely expanding the existing program tactics.

You should focus on innovative new techniques that will generate an estimated dollar ROI from ad conversion, the high dollar value of media publicity, new visitors produced for the destination through Internet programming, new sales programs resulting from co-op partnership efforts, etc.

5. Answer the Questions that Stand in Your Way

You will have a lot of publics to cover and favorably influence, including the general public, the media, government, and stakeholders. A planned effort requires that you initially determine the principal, specific interests of each of them, and then produce frequently asked questions to answer and assuage their individual concerns. For example:

- **The general public may be interested in knowing** how this program is useful for them by providing new visitor taxes that can help support the community and minimize resident taxes and produce new amenities and lifestyle attributes for their enjoyment, etc.
- **Government may question:** When do we reach the point of dimin-

ished ROI of this program? Actually, the opposite should occur—and the ROI in visitor receipts and benefits over time should grow higher. This is because a byproduct of success should be additional infra-structure of new visitor facilities such as accommodations, retail, and restaurants. Also, the branding effort from this enhanced program will build marketing communications equity for the long term and assist in delivering even greater returns from marketing, as new business partners also work to leverage additional marketing efforts under your DMO umbrella effort.

6. Build a Strong Team Effort for Launching

You and your staff, along with board input, will judge how to most effectively launch this effort. There's usually a special task force assigned to the task, with representation from key constituents, to manage or plan the process with over-sight from the board and CEO. That may sometimes be supported by special guid-ance and counsel from a lobbyist that's close to the government officials required for support, a local PR firm, or others as the needs require. Above all, make it an inclusionary, collaborative process. For example:

- **New York City:** When the new funding plan for the New York CVB budget was launched, it was titled "A Vital Investment for Economic Growth in New York City." It was formally supported by a wide range of leadership partners that helped assure passage. They included the New York Hotel Association, the New York Restaurant Association, Associa-tion for a Better New York, and the New York Society of Association Executives. We also hired top lobbyists and PR support.

- **Door County, Wisconsin:** The board of the CVB mounted a successful campaign for the hotel TOT that focused on each individual village. It has produced new annual funding that has dramatically grown from $700,000 to about $3 million—and its efforts are all targeted on deliv-ering strong ROI for the destination.

- **Ann Arbor, Michigan:** Under the leadership of CEO Mary Kerr, the CVB board rallied to develop an innovative campaign that increased its annual budget by 150 percent, thanks to a comprehensive new plan that influenced favorable opinion and the stellar reputation of the CVB with elected officials.

- **Myrtle Beach, Charleston, and Hilton Head, South Carolina:** New marketing programs were produced with the ongoing voluntary support of the hotel communities that increased their community

DMO marketing budgets from between several hundred thousand dollars to several millions in new programming. That local funding was then matched fifty cents on the dollar by the state tourism office.

Your destination's future success is based on your performance-based programs, the funding that delivers them and solid community support for implementation. Be sure to employ strong action plan recommendations, like the next example, which delivers significant, positive results.

A Strong ROI Case History for Funding Development

Funding development plans usually gain far greater acceptability in today's business environment when they are highlighted by exciting major marketing initiatives that can guarantee and produce significant economic returns.

None, in our judgment, is as effective in that regard as the eBrains Inc. Internet solution for delivering thousands of new visitors and resulting room nights—and producing at least a 40-to-1 ROI in marketing dollars and a 6-to-1 tax revenue return on marketing dollars.

Here's how it has worked for more than fifty state, regional, and local DMOs:

Web visitors to a cross-section of travel-related websites see a specially produced branded travel offering from the travel destination being featured. When visitors are invited to inquire, they receive a specially produced, electronic publication about the destination's diversity of attractions, events, accommodations, restaurant/retail, and other offerings. Inquiries are also screened to assure that the DMO receives only highly qualified, actionable inquiries.

As consumers are taken through the cycle of destination awareness, interest, and desire to visit, they subsequently make the purchase decision; and the results later documented through third-party conversion research analysis are substantial.

With a marketing program purchase of $500,000, for example:

- The destination is guaranteed highly qualified inquirers at a cost of $2 each.
- Fully 15 percent of these inquirers, amounting to 37,500 visitor parties, are then guaranteed to convert to actual visits and deliver about 180,000 room nights.

- This produces an estimated total economic impact to the community exceeding $30 million—a 60-to-1 visitor spending ROI, and a 7-to-1 tax revenue return from the initial $500,000 Internet marketing investment.
- Conversion to actual visitors is then tracked for the DMO using conversion technology licensed and administered by Texas A&M University research.

For more information, contact Ralph Thompson, president and chief brain, eBrains Inc., at rthompson@ebrainsinc.com or 703-303-2252.

Casino Gaming and Its Positive Impacts for Destination Marketing

With casinos coming soon to a neighborhood near you—or certainly within easy reach—many destination marketers are asking themselves: what's the potential impact of gaming on our industry?

When Harrah's Entertainment Inc. and the Narragansett Indians proposed a casino hotel facility in West Warwick, Rhode Island, major tourism leaders led by the governor balked.

The facility's 115,000 square feet of casino space, five hundred hotel rooms, two full-service restaurants, and a 55,000-square-foot ballroom would do considerable damage to the state and local tourism industry, many said.

In response, Harrah's asked me to present testimony to committees of the Rhode Island Legislature to factually address a number of relevant issues. The information we produced at that time should also provide useful background for you regarding casino gaming and its positive impacts for destination marketing.

Since the development of Foxwoods Casino in nearby Connecticut, a steady stream of Rhode Island residents had been motivated to visit there for leisure travel and meetings—taking millions of travel dollars outside Rhode Island that could have supported local jobs and added tax revenue. In fact, according to Foxwoods executives, many Rhode Island businesses had taken their meetings to Foxwoods.

This isn't surprising. As tourism has become America's number-one industry, the attraction of casino gaming and its additional amenities for meetings, restaurants, retail, and entertainment have become major parts of the product marketing mix that influence millions of visitor travel decisions throughout the United States.

What is surprising, however, was the dialogue and concerns expressed by some local tourism interests who believed that this proposed new venue from Harrah's and the Narragansett Indians would have limited or negated opportunities for tourism growth and resulting economic prosperity for Rhode Island and the Providence Warwick area. Indeed, the opposite is true, and this has been consistently so in destination after tourism destination throughout the United States.

To address these negative concerns, we first listed each of them, and then responded with the opinions from many of America's top tourism development experts.

Concern 1. The new casino will compete with the state's hotels, convention centers, and other tourism attractions.

Actually, the opposite would occur. This new casino facility would provide a new, major motivational reason for travelers to visit Rhode Island and the Providence Warwick area and extend length of stay.

In fact, fully two out of three visits (69%) to the new casino were projected to be from out-of-state visitors, according to business analysis from Business Research and Economic Advisors (A. J. Moody, *The Economic Impact of the Proposed Destination Casino in West Warwick, RI*, March 2003). This creates a growing market for new travelers to Rhode Island that would use, over time, still more hotel rooms—not less.

Because the casino provides more consumer travel choices—and enhances the visitor product—it would also help the destination effectively compete with other out-of-state destinations, such as Foxwoods and the Mohegan Sun. It would also heighten the destination's appeal and provide broader diversity of the visitor destination for such feeder markets as Boston.

We asked nationally recognized tourism expert John Boatright, chairman emeritus of the Association of Travel Marketing Executives, about this issue:

> Think of destination-selling as you would a major retail mall. Most visitors don't just come for one store in a mall. They come for the whole experience, the variety of different stores, products, and appeals, and the more product diversification there is in a mall—as with a tourism community—the more potential visitors will be attracted. That's the way it is with destination marketing. Diversity of tour product brings more visitors, and this new casino product will deliver an expanded visitor draw for Providence Warwick and the entire State of Rhode Island.

Throughout America's tourism industry, experts conclude that the addition of casino gaming creates a positive visitor amenity that ultimately brings new visitor business—not diminishes or dilutes it.

A prime example is Memphis, Tennessee, where tourism is now a multibillion-dollar contributor to the healthy regional economy. As neighboring Tunica, Mississippi, has become one of America's most successful gaming capitals, it has had positive impacts in producing incremental business for Memphis and its visitor industry, according to local experts.

"We're a much better travel destination today because of Tunica's nearby Casino Gaming market," said Memphis Convention and Visitor Bureau President & CEO Kevin Kane. "It has added diversity to our product mix and ultimately brought more visitors and more visitor dollars here that have benefited everyone—particularly the creation of much-needed jobs for the hotel and restaurant sectors."

Casinos provide another visitor amenity that can both motivate visitors and fulfill their interests while visiting destinations because of the increased worldwide popularity of gaming entertainment. Thus, by providing new visitors to the state, more visitors would be on-site to see and do more. And Rhode Island and the Providence Warwick area would, over time, significantly increase their relative market share of the New England visitor industry.

According to Bob Whitley, late president of the US Tour Operators Association, whose members produce the majority of tourism programs sold internationally:

> Travelers just about everywhere have gotten used to the proposition that casino gaming is now just minutes away from most destinations. And many consider it another amenity, another thing to do that enhances the visitor experience.

In addition, for those future repeat out-of-state visitors to Providence and Warwick who extend their stay by visiting the new casino facility, the beneficiaries would be other area restaurants, retail, and attractions who also make a portion of their living serving travelers.

Concern 2. The new casino will draw customers away from the state-owned Rhode Island Convention Center and area hotels.

No. Actually more meeting and convention planners would begin to choose Rhode Island and the Providence Warwick area. Throughout the meeting/convention industry, planners who choose various meeting venues for their individual conventions and meetings employ a great diversity of site selection criteria based on the individual needs of their associations and members.

According to Joel Dolci, president/CEO of the New York Society of Association Executives, whose 2,000-plus members conduct many meetings in the Northeast:

> Meeting planners aren't all looking for the same thing. Some will choose a casino property, while others will prefer a public facility. You have to understand that there's a lot of potential meeting business out there, so the more meeting venue choices a community has to offer, the greater the potential volume. This casino should bring more meeting business to Rhode Island—not take away business from other existing facilities.

This thought is echoed by Jeff Vasser, president of the Atlantic City Convention and Visitors Authority, which operates Atlantic City's convention center:

> There's a good synergism here and in Las Vegas between the principal government-operated city convention center and the meeting and

convention facilities of the casinos. The end result is more business for everybody—not less. That's just the way the business works. What's more, there are thousands of non-casino hotel rooms that are filled daily from the attraction of the casino industry. It's truly a business partnership.

That means additional meeting business for Rhode Island. And when the delegates and their spouses are finished with the work at hand, the casino will offer strong entertainment potential for many who may not have previously chosen Providence/Warwick as a meeting site.

Concern 3. The addition of five hundred new hotel rooms associated with the casino would negatively impact occupancy rates of existing hotels.

In the short term, when any new hotel facility opens in a community, there is the potential for a corresponding modest, temporary reduction in the hotel occupancy of existing properties.

However, at the same time, the total number of occupied hotel rooms throughout the community generally increases, producing more visitors and visitor receipts for the destination. Then as additional visitor amenities attract more travelers, the community's hotel occupancy will continue to increase.

There is another positive factor, too. When the new casino begins to produce new business for its hotel property, it will also generate overflow that will be absorbed by many existing hotel properties. And other visitors motivated to come to Rhode Island to enjoy the casino will have a variety of hotel accommodations to choose from—thus supporting the entire hospitality community.

Concern 4. A large-scale casino like Harrah's would drain the state's established hospitality industry (quality service employees), giving Rhode Island a bad name.

Not according to the Hotel and Restaurant Workers International. There are about 61,000 hospitality employee positions employed throughout the state. Even if all new casino jobs were filled from the existing industry labor pool—certainly an unlikely event—it would amount to only about 10 percent of current positions.

Actually, the casino will produce another 6,700 important jobs both on-site and as a direct result of the project. And management will also put in place an extensive job-training program to provide enhanced skill sets for entry-level positions.

Concern 5. Casino development will have a negative effect on the vitality of the local restaurant industry.

This concern has proven to be unfounded in jurisdiction after jurisdiction where the issue has been examined based on empirical and unbiased research.

Drs. George Fenich and Kathryn Hashimoto of the University of New Orleans

School of Hotel, Restaurant, and Tourism Administration have studied the impact of casinos on local restaurants in locations throughout the United States, from small rural towns to large urban arenas. They found that although some individual operators experience problems, the industry as a whole thrives and grows with increases in the number of establishments and employees and higher rates of pay; a variation of the old saying: "A rising tide floats all seaworthy ships"(Fenich & Hashimoto, *Perceptions of Cannibalization: What Is the Real Effect of Casinos on Restaurants?* University of New Orleans, 2000).

We also spoke with Steven Richer, then executive director of the Mississippi Gulf Coast Convention and Visitors Bureau about the effect of casinos on non-casino businesses. Richer has witnessed the results first-hand in three major gaming jurisdictions as the former executive director of the Nevada Convention and Tourism Commission and the past president of the Atlantic City Convention and Visitors Bureau:

> Wherever there is an already established tourism product, a casino facility creates an added amenity that enhances the attractiveness of the area and gives people another reason to visit. It invariably results in more business for everyone—restaurants, hotels, shops—you name it. It's a catalyst for development, not a deterrent.

According to Jim Funk, retired executive vice president and CEO of the Louisiana Restaurant Association, casino restaurants would not be a negative factor for the existing restaurant industry of Rhode Island. In Louisiana's case, the state perceived the need for casinos to level the tourism playing field with neighboring Mississippi, which already had casinos. Referring to the experience in New Orleans, Funk remarked:

> At first our local restaurants were concerned about cheap food and competition from the casino. In fact, this association was instrumental in obtaining restrictions on their food and beverage operations. But, over time, we found the tight restrictions were just not necessary. You see, the casinos don't just give away their food to everybody and they really can't compete with the great food and diverse menus of our local restaurants.

From Shreveport/Bossier City to Lake Charles, the local restaurant industry in Louisiana has been expanding. In each case, Funk said:

> The casinos have brought more visitors and the local restaurant industry is booming. Unemployment is down and property values are up. The people are glad casinos are here.

For all of these reasons, there should have been no cause to believe that the effect of a casino in the Providence/Warwick area would be any different than it has been in other parts of the country—producing more visitors, more jobs, better wages, and an expanding local restaurant industry.

Forging Effective DMO Gaming Partnerships

For those communities with gaming partners, or future plans to create them, we recommend development of a strong business relationship to maximize success.

Because the marketing model for casino gaming enterprises would most likely concentrate on the local and regional market, a partnership with the DMO will expand the casino's marketing reach and resulting opportunity for new patrons and revenue.

For the DMO, the casino will provide diversification of product and visitor interest. In fact, with exception of retail shopping, casino gaming has become the United States' most popular visitor activity.

Potential joint initiatives may include

- **destination advertising initiatives,** including co-op ad placement, special consumer sections in magazines and newspapers, direct mail, etc.
- **media publicity programs,** including promotional assistance, the hosting of writer familiarizations and site inspections, on the road receptions showcasing the destination, along with sales blitzes in major feeder markets, etc.
- **sales bookings** made by the casino
- **web marketing,** including DMO website banner advertising, special mentions, web linkage, etc.
- **trade show participation** and support for the meetings and travel trade sectors
- **DMO publications** for distribution through the casino
- **any other major promotions** recommended.

The DMO would then provide the casino

- **editorial coverage** in appropriate consumer and meeting/travel trade publications
- **appropriate listings** in DMO-produced publications (official visitor guide, tour operator and meeting planner guides, convention services directory)
- **sales leads** for tour group and meetings business
- **other materials** including upcoming convention/event lists, convention sales updates

- **brochure distribution** at the visitor center and other dissemination programs.

Creation of such a strong partnership alliance will provide additional manpower and financial contributions to the DMO, along with increased marketing support.

The results should assure a new and productive travel industry relationship that leverages higher volumes of new visitor business for the community and strengthens the DMO and its future marketing efforts.

Is New Alternative Funding on Your Horizon? The Tourism BID

Many DMOs are currently facing a financial crunch due to inflationary factors and subsequent funding reductions. This situation has led many to seek out potentially new, stable funding sources for the vital destination marketing services they provide—and many are now investigating tourism business improvement districts for this purpose.

What is a tourism improvement district, how will it work for my destination, and how do we create it? For those answers, we turned to the experts in this field, Civitas Advisors of Sacramento, California, the acknowledged industry leader in tourism business improvement district (TBID) formation. The firm's founder and president, Attorney John Lambeth, was the primary author of California's latest law allowing TBID formation. Civitas has worked with forty-two of California's sixty tourism improvement districts (TIDs) and specializes in all aspects of the formation and renewal processes. Here is Lambeth's directional guidance for all DMOs.

TIDs are a stable funding source for destination marketing efforts. TIDs are typically funded by an assessment on hotel room sales, which is designed to tie tourism marketing funds directly to the lodging industry. The funds are collected by the local jurisdiction with TOTs and passed on to a designated nonprofit corporation. Typically, the designated nonprofit is a convention and visitors bureau or similar DMO, or a new corporation set up by businesses specifically to manage the district funds.

California has been the leader in the TID phenomenon, with over sixty local districts in cities like San Diego, Los Angeles, and Hollywood, plus a statewide district. West Hollywood pioneered the TID concept in 1992, igniting a revolution that sparked formation of TIDs throughout California. Ranging from small five-hotel districts to supersized districts with 350 hotels, with budgets from $100,000 to $30 million, in coastal havens and urban enclaves, California's local TIDs represent every type and size of destination. Throughout California, local TIDs raise in excess of $125 million for marketing programs.

How Is a Tourism Improvement District Formed?

In addition to California, three other states have enacted legislation allowing TID formation: Washington, Montana, and Texas. There are ten districts in Washington and eight in Montana. Texas's law is so new that no districts have yet been finalized, but at least one is in the works. A few more states are exploring potential TID legislation; yet others need a gentle push in that direction. Enacting legislation, or identifying existing legislation, is the initial step toward forming a TID. TID legislation typically delineates a formation process with business owner and government approval mechanisms, describes procedures for assessment collection and budgeting, and sets requirements for district activities and management.

Once legislation is in place, the TID formation process follows a typical pattern. The five-step formation process begins with forming a project steering committee, undertakes outreach and approval processes, and ends with forming the district:

- **Step One: Form a Steering Committee.** Like any project, the TID formation process needs a steady hand to guide it to success. A project steering committee should be assembled at the outset of the formation process, including DMO staff, business owners, local government representatives, and other supportive parties. This steering committee will work with consultants, other business owners, and government staff to make the district reality. Throughout the formation process, the steering committee will develop communications materials to reach out to business owners, such as this FAQ sheet developed for the Napa Valley Tourism Improvement District (www.legendarynapavalley.com/docs/1_NVTBID%20FAQs%20and%20Timeline.pdf).

- **Step Two: Create a Database.** The steering committee's first task will be to assemble a database of businesses that will be in the district. Database information includes business owner name, business address, gross revenue (where available), and other characteristics of the business. The database is the foundation of the TID formation process and is often updated and modified throughout the project.

- **Step Three: Develop a Business Plan.** Through outreach to business owners, the steering committee can identify district needs and priorities. TIDs can fund many types of destination marketing programs, including advertising campaigns, sales lead generation, website development and marketing, social-media marketing, and special event sponsorship. The business plan will identify the services to be provided and include a proposed assessment rate and budget to implement those services. The business plan should also include a description of the district area and a list of businesses in the district.

- **Step Four: Owner Approval Process.** Many business owners are attracted to the TID concept because they have a measure of control over the district, especially in district formation. The owner approval process varies by jurisdiction, but often includes either a petition or ballot process. In whatever manner local legislation calls for, business owners will have an opportunity to approve the proposed district and associated business plan.

- *Step Five: Local Government Approval Process.* The final step in TID formation is local government approval. Typically, the local government entity will examine and approve the district plan, certify that enough business owners support the district, and officially order formation of the district.

Case Study: San Diego Tourism Marketing District

Sunny San Diego, California, may not seem like a destination in need of a TID. In fact, you had probably visited San Diego long before it created a TID in 2007. But, what you may not know is that the San Diego tourism industry began suffering from a diminishing availability of public funds for destination marketing in the early 2000s. By 2003, San Diego's lodging industry was actively investigating alternative methods of funding marketing programs. After dozens of meetings to consider their options, lodging businesses decided to create a TID. In 2005, a consultant was hired and TID formation began.

Following the typical TID formation pattern, a steering committee was designated to guide the project. Over two years, the steering committee and consultant worked with the City of San Diego to secure adoption of an ordinance allowing TID formation (a method of enacting enabling legislation available in some jurisdictions), reached out to lodging business owners, and successfully navigated the city approval process. In 2007, the committee's efforts resulted in formation of the San Diego Tourism Marketing District (www.sdtmd.org/about).

Since 2007, the San Diego Tourism Marketing District has provided more than $25 million a year in marketing funds to the San Diego Convention and Visitors Bureau, the San Diego Film Commission, the San Diego Sports Commission, and numerous other tourism-related organizations. With the TID as a stable funding force for destination marketing, the San Diego CVB successfully launched the hugely popular "Happy Happens" (www.youtube.com/user/visitsandiego) advertising campaign.

Will Your Destination Create the Next TID?

The TID concept has proven its effectiveness in creating a stable source of funding for tourism promotion. Recognizing the funding advantage a TID can provide, industry experts all over the world have taken the future into their own hands by creating TIDs. Industry experts have come to realize forming a district may be the single-most significant tool available to create a long-term impact on tourism promotion financing.

For the latest information, contact John Lambeth, Esq., president, Civitas Advisors, at www.civitasadvisors.com; 7700 College Town Drive, Suite 111, Sacramento, CA 95826; 800-999-7781; or Jlambeth@civitasadvisors.com.

Preserving Tourism

Graffiti, pollution, vandalism, and litter—just a few of the plagues that adversely affect a growing number of worldwide tourism sites—not just today, but for generations to come. How's our preservation scorecard? Not great. So what part can each of us play in dealing with this daunting issue?

"Please pack out your trash!" the public signs implore trekkers at major outdoor recreational areas worldwide. Yet noted destinations, from Africa's Mt. Kilimanjaro to Japan's Mt. Fuji, continue to be strewn with heaps of unsightly litter from the uncaring.

On the other side of the world in Peru's Inca city of Machu Picchu and Mexico's ancient Maya city of Chichen Itza, some have defiled these revered sites, using them as public bathrooms and chiseling their initials deep into the precious stonework.

There's also the tragic looting of rare antiquities in Iraq following the outbreak of war when treasured historic sites were left unprotected from vandalism and theft.

While all of this is unacceptable, there's much more environmental undoing now at work in a different, more subtle way.

Years ago, an international travel writer from France was invited to visit one of America's premier regions, the Amish country of the east, replete with a quaint, simpler way of life where visitors could step back to a time before electricity, autos, and the like—just shoofly pie, horse and carriage travel, and pastoral, picturesque scenery. Following the writer's visit, and upon her return home, she received a call from the destination official. "How was it?" the writer was asked. "It simply wasn't there anymore," she replied sadly.

Where once had been a delightful and pristine environment, auto visitors soon began arriving in greater numbers, she surmised. Then gas stations followed as did roadside motels, frozen custard stands, burger drive-ins, new tourist rides, other children entertainments, a wax museum, and assorted other attractions.

I'm sure you can name numerous other examples where people in our industry have popularized destinations and, by so doing over time, have actually contributed to the slow demise of their inherent charm and resulting diminished popularity for future generations of visitors.

Fortunately, many communities are now initiating new zoning and regulations to protect and preserve. Ecotourism and sustainable tourism programs are gaining more support by travelers.

Impacts on World Tourism

Unfortunately, the need is great and time may be running out for some destinations and sites.

Global economists are now forecasting continued international tourism growth in the 3–6 percent range annually, depending on the location. And this continuous growth is anticipated to place great stress on a number of sites that support mass tourism.

You've surely heard about the New Seven Wonders of the World, announced several years ago following a global poll to decide a new list of human-made marvels. The winners were voted for by Internet and phone, *American Idol*–style.

They included the 105-foot-tall Christ the Redeemer statue in Rio de Janeiro, Brazil, the Coliseum in Rome, India's Taj Mahal, the Great Wall of China, Jordan's ancient city of Petra, Machu Picchu, and Chichén Itzá. The contest was organized by the New7Wonders Foundation—the brainchild of Swiss filmmaker and museum curator Bernard Weber—in order to "protect humankind's heritage across the globe." The foundation says the poll attracted almost a hundred million votes.

Yet the competition has proved controversial, drawing criticism from the United Nations' cultural organization UNESCO, which administers the World Heritage sites program. "This initiative cannot, in any significant and sustainable manner, contribute to the preservation of sites elected by [the] public," UNESCO said in a recent statement.

Perhaps not. But it will surely spark new levels of awareness for these spectacular wonders—and that's a good thing if preservation steps can assure that visitors will treat these treasures more respectfully, which hasn't always been the case. So what's the long-term answer? More focus on the traveler's behavior would be a good start.

In this regard, the International Institute for Peace through Tourism now promotes the Credo of the Peaceful Traveler that offers thoughts for visitors to keep in mind on their journeys.

This credo eloquently states what we should indeed require from travelers. It's a thoughtful pledge, and one that should be endorsed and communicated by the tourism and travel industry organizations of the world.

Taking it a step farther, shouldn't such a signed pledge also be adopted as a prerequisite for visitation to many environmentally critical sites?

Credo of the Peaceful Traveler

Grateful for the opportunity to travel and experience the world,
and because peace begins with the individual, I affirm my
personal responsibility and commitment to:
Journey with an open mind and gentle heart
Accept with grace and gratitude the diversity I encounter
Revere and protect the natural environment which sustains all life
Appreciate all cultures I discover
Respect and thank my hosts for their welcome
Offer my hand in friendship to everyone I meet
Support travel services that share these views and act upon
them and,
By my spirit, words, and actions, encourage others to travel
the world in peace.

Action Is Needed

However, stabilizing and assuring environmental integrity throughout the tourism industry requires more than just pledges. It demands action.

Some believe that the real inherent issue is that the world's population is growing so fast that we are using the earth's resources faster than they can be replenished.

"The opportunity for the world's tourism industry," according to travel expert John Boatright, "is to symbolically raise a big banner and carry it high and proud, to make our industry an agent for awareness and change, and this needs to happen before we are accused of being the problem—or at least part of it."

Finally, we come to the most disturbing concern: Rising seas from global warming, which experts tell us will alter our world in this century. These waters, aided by sinking land, threaten to submerge Bangkok, Thailand's capital of more than 10 million people—and this is just one of a number of large cities at risk of being swamped as sea levels continue to rise in coming decades, according to warnings at the recent Intergovernmental Panel on Climate Change held there.

The loss of Bangkok would destroy the country's economic engine and a major hub for regional tourism, experts warned.

The Public Appears Skeptical

What's appalling is that the general public doesn't seem to believe these forecasts about ominous impacts of global warming.

In one AOL Internet poll of about 30,000 participants, only 38 percent said they trusted these long-term forecasts, while another 38 percent said they believed them "just a little," and the remaining 24 percent said they believed them "not at all." And when asked: are you concerned about how climate changes will affect the area in which you live, fully 40 percent of respondents said "no."

I suspect that an additional survey of just those people who said they believed these concerns would also confirm that many of them are complacent—thinking that the human race is simply incapable of doing anything about this future plight. If true, that would be very sad.

What Should Be Our Industry's Response?

Isn't it time for the tourism industry to publicly respond and be a part of a new dialogue on this critical subject?

I recommended that our tourism industry associations work cooperatively to develop such an action plan grounded in these two key points:

- **Make a critical assessment of this issue** by quantifying the potentially destructive consequences to the world's tourism industry and those it serves.
- **Provide a pragmatic, inclusionary plan** that tourism industry officials and business partners everywhere can embrace and participate in to preserve our visitor resources and amenities for new generations to come.

Tourism belongs to everybody. But just saying it won't make it so. Perhaps we can find common ground for consensus action, because we certainly need it, don't we?

The Future of Destination Marketing: Final Observations and Challenges

This book wouldn't be finished without a few personal observations about where our DMO culture is going and how it can aspire to even greater success.

What are the DMO's greatest challenges, and how do we solve them?

According to the 2008 Futures Study from DMAI, the top three DMO challenges are relevance, the value proposition, and visibility. That's probably quite accurate. But I'm a firm believer that we shouldn't worry too much about things we cannot change—and there are some aspects of DMO relevance and value that fall into that category; case in point, the issue of "disintermediation" from third-party competitors such as Orbitz, Travelocity, and Priceline. So instead, for the next industry strategic planning initiative, I recommend an optimistic visioning process that deals with the development of practical solutions for DMO industry success.

Then where should our focus be?

DMOs should be more entrepreneurial. In Atlantic City, our staff developed the Travel Media Showcase. But only a handful of other DMOs have made inroads in developing tradeshow and visitor-related profit centers. Other opportunities for gaining industry relevance and value are certainly out there. We also need to concentrate on the DMO's key strengths for our communities, making sure that our objectives (see chapter 1) are being maximized. Let's also work to galvanize community and government partnerships through greater collaboration that raises the visibility and role of the DMO and the destination's tourism industry it serves. Local advocacy and product development opportunities should be key DMO future considerations, too.

So how would you describe our future need in one word?

Performance. It is only through performance—primarily quantitative productivity performance directly achieved from DMO program initiatives—that we will further enhance our value, visibility, and reputation for excellence.

Aren't we moving in that direction?

Absolutely. But when most DMO/government contracts and public reporting don't include in-depth quantifiable performance goals and productivity to be achieved by them, we still have a long way to go.

What else needs addressing?

Professionalism. We also forget at times that we are professional destination marketers—friendly competitors—who are in the marketplace trying to generate greater market share at the expense of other DMO competitors. For the most part, it's a finite consumer market out there, and we are all vying for a segment of it. That's why most of our processes, marketing plans, and research should be considered proprietary and not openly shared with other destinations—yet many do it willingly. Perhaps it is because they're proud of the work they've accomplished. But can you imagine Coca-Cola openly discussing their marketing plans with Pepsi-Cola or Apple sharing with Samsung? Maturing this competitive posture in the DMO industry would be a giant step in the right direction.

Any other thoughts about the future needs of tourism?

Here are several observations:

- **A New CVB Management Model**—Some industry observers have forecast that in the future clusters of DMOs may be managed by one firm, not unlike convention center management companies, to save costs for goods and services while assuring uniform advancement in necessary personnel management and marketing skills. But instead, it is the marketing requirement of the DMOs culture—and the inherent responsibility for turning a profit and ROI for the community in relationship to other competitors—that will assure that this is not likely to ever occur as a viable trend.

- **Advocating for Tourism**—There is a growing need for local, regional, and national advocacy on behalf of our industry associations, particularly in the area of taxation to the visitor without representation that diverts funds from tourism marketing. Unfortunately, when this situation occurs and bed tax funds are instead provided to the general fund for other government needs like park maintenance, arena development, or police/fire/social services, this further adversely reduces the tourism industry's long-term benefits in bringing more visitors and visitor expenditures to the community. Greater advocacy from industry leaders would also provide greater visibility for the industry's ongoing importance in job generation and social benefits provided through tourism.

- **Recommending the Best Model for CVBs**—Finally, the optimum DMO has emerged as a nonprofit association management model with more than two-thirds of CVBs establishing this structure, which has significant benefits compared to the previous government or chamber-oriented DMO. Industry association leadership should take a new step forward by providing counsel and advice to emerging destinations in avoiding pitfalls as they seek to produce the best DMO model for their communities.

CONCLUSION

I couldn't find a better way to conclude this book than by sharing my favorite and most inspiring travel quotes.

Hopefully, they'll also vividly remind you of travel's far-reaching effects on people and why so many are destined to work in this wonderful business of tourism. Many of these quotations also give inspiration and guidance to our daily tasks of marketing to the consumer: fulfilling their travel interests and desires through the destinations we represent and serve.

Finally, the very best wishes to you on your personal journey ahead.

"The world is a book and those who do not travel read only one page."
–St. Augustine

"The use of traveling is to regulate imagination by reality, and instead of thinking how things may be, to see them as they are."
–Samuel Johnson

"All the pathos and irony of leaving one's youth behind is thus implicit in every joyous moment of travel: one knows that the first joy can never be recovered, and the wise traveler learns not to repeat successes but tries new places all the time."
–Paul Fussell

"Travel is fatal to prejudice, bigotry, and narrow-mindedness."
–Mark Twain

"He who does not travel does not know the value of men."
–Moorish proverb

"People travel to faraway places to watch, in fascination, the kind of people they ignore at home."
–Dagobert D. Runes

"A journey is like marriage. The certain way to be wrong is to think you control it."

–John Steinbeck

"No one realizes how beautiful it is to travel until he comes home and rests his head on his old, familiar pillow."

–Lin Yutang

"For my part, I travel not to go anywhere, but to go. I travel for travel's sake. The great affair is to move."

– Robert Louis Stevenson

"One's destination is never a place, but a new way of seeing things."

–Henry Miller

"A traveler without observation is a bird without wings."

–Moslih Eddin Saadi

"When we get out of the glass bottle of our ego and when we escape like the squirrels in the cage of our personality and get into the forest again, we shall shiver with cold and fright. But things will happen to us so that we don't know ourselves. Cool, unlying life will rush in."

–D. H. Lawrence

"To awaken quite alone in a strange town is one of the pleasantest sensations in the world."

–Freya Stark

"Twenty years from now you will be more disappointed by the things you didn't do than by the ones you did do. So throw off the bowlines, sail away from the safe harbor. Catch the trade winds in your sails. Explore. Dream. Discover."

–Mark Twain

"Travel is more than the seeing of sights; it is a change that goes on, deep and permanent, in the ideas of living."

–Miriam Beard

"All journeys have secret destinations of which the traveler is unaware."

–Martin Buber

"We live in a wonderful world that is full of beauty, charm and adventure. There is no end to the adventures we can have if only we seek them with our eyes open."

–Jawaharial Nehru

"Tourists don't know where they've been, travelers don't know where they're going."

–Paul Theroux

"Do not follow where the path may lead. Go instead where there is no path and leave a trail."

–Ralph Waldo Emerson

"Two roads diverged in a wood and I took the one less traveled by."

–Robert Frost

"A journey of a thousand miles must begin with a single step."

–Lao Tzu

"There is no moment of delight in any pilgrimage like the beginning of it."

–Charles Dudley Warner

"A good traveler has no fixed plans and is not intent on arriving."

–Lao Tzu

"If you reject the food, ignore the customs, fear the religion and avoid the people, you might better stay at home."

–James Michener

"The journey not the arrival matters."

–T. S. Eliot

"Not all those who wander are lost."

–J. R. R. Tolkien

"Perhaps travel cannot prevent bigotry, but by demonstrating that all people cry, laugh, eat, worry, and die, it can introduce the idea that if we try and understand each other, we may even become friends."

–Maya Angelou

"A journey is best measured in friends, rather than miles."

–Tim Cahill

"Wandering re-establishes the original harmony which once existed between man and the universe."

–Anatole France

"Travel and change of place impart new vigor to the mind."

–Seneca

"The whole object of travel is not to set foot on foreign land; it is at last to set foot on one's own country as a foreign land."

–G. K. Chesterton

"Like all great travelers, I have seen more than I remember, and remember more than I have seen."

–Benjamin Disraeli

ABOUT THE AUTHOR

Marshall Murdaugh has been helping travel destinations become more successful for more than three decades—first as the president and CEO for some of the United States' best recognized destination marketing programs, including Virginia State Tourism (1970–83), the Memphis Convention and Visitors Bureau (1984–87), the New York City Convention and Visitors Bureau (1988–94), Atlantic City (1994–2000)—and as marketing and strategic planning consultant to more than eighty city, state, and regional destinations, tourism-related businesses, corporations, and travel organizations.

Throughout his career, Murdaugh has developed dozens of multimillion-dollar program initiatives including destination advertising, meetings/convention sales, Internet development, public relations and media publicity, and other performance-based, award-winning marketing programs for tourism destinations. And his ground-breaking brand development work for "Virginia Is for Lovers," "New York, the Big Apple," and other memorable marketing campaigns have consistently brought multibillion-dollar business results to dozens of communities throughout the industry.

His client list has included such diverse destinations as Acapulco, Miami, Newport Beach, Palm Springs, Pittsburgh, Puerto Rico, Niagara Falls, the Black Hills and Badlands of South Dakota, the Pocono Mountains of Pennsylvania, Los Angeles, Baltimore, Hilton Head Island, Myrtle Beach, Savannah, Steuben County's Finger Lakes, Atlantic City, Natchitoches, Louisiana, Florida's Space Coast, and Mexico City.

Murdaugh also serves as senior strategic planning consultant to SMG, the industry's premiere private management company for public facilities, including convention centers, arenas, and stadiums.

Recognized for his development of performance-driven marketing, Murdaugh was a principal contributor on the performance team that developed the convention/tourism industry's marketing performance standards and return-on-investment criteria for the Destination Marketing Association International.

He is the recipient of the Lifetime Career Achievement Award from the Association of Travel Marketing executives, as well as its former chairman. He also served as special consultant to the Visit USA Program for federal tourism marketing and received the US Department of Commerce's First Special Citation for Distinguished Service.

Murdaugh was a member of the board of the International Association of CVBs, the US Travel Industry Association of America, and the New York Society of Association Executives and chairman of two major US regional tourism marketing organizations: Travel South USA of the eleven southern states and the Washington DC/Central Atlantic States Travel Council.

He received his BFA degree from Virginia Commonwealth University and later served as a member of the adjunct faculty where he taught commercial recreation and tourism for seven years. He is also a frequent presenter and lecturer for numerous tourism conferences, seminars, and workshops worldwide.

Murdaugh's *Performance Self-Assessment Manual for CVBs* has been employed by DMOs globally and is considered a major industry resource, and his e-marketing newsletter for global tourism executives is available on the web at www.MMTourismMarketing.com.

He continues his destination consultancy assignments as the principal of Marshall Murdaugh Marketing and resides in his hometown of Richmond, Virginia.

In his spare time, Marshall is an enthusiast and participant in global adventure travel and serves on the Board of Trustees of the US Amateur Boxing Foundation.